HAL LEONARD

HANDPAN METHOD

BY MARK D'AMBROSIO
& JENNY ROBINSON

Photographer: Jon Hain
Editor/Contributor: Alison Mikulyuk

To access video visit:
www.halleonard.com/mylibrary

Enter Code
1447-3846-3516-1848

ISBN 978-1-5400-4431-0

Visit Hal Leonard Online at
www.halleonard.com

Contact us:
Hal Leonard
7777 West Bluemound Road
Milwaukee, WI 53213
Email: info@halleonard.com

In Europe, contact:
Hal Leonard Europe Limited
42 Wigmore Street
Marylebone, London, W1U 2RN
Email: info@halleonardeurope.com

In Australia, contact:
Hal Leonard Australia Pty. Ltd.
4 Lentara Court
Cheltenham, Victoria, 3192 Australia
Email: info@halleonard.com.au

CONTENTS

INTRODUCTION

A handpan is a musical instrument made of steel and played with the hands. Handpans are formed by two bowl-shaped sheets of steel fastened together to create a resonant sound chamber. The sonority of the handpan has an affective quality that some describe as ethereal or otherworldly. Most handpans have a relatively small number of notes tuned to a single key, making them accessible to those just learning music, while also being versatile and complex enough to challenge and inspire even the most accomplished musicians.

The handpan is one of the few new acoustic instruments developed in the 21st century. The first of these instruments were designed and produced in Switzerland in the early 2000s, but the handpan can trace its origins to the steelpan instruments developed in Trinidad and Tobago in the 1940s and other percussive and resonating instruments. While the approach to playing the handpan is a bit different from a traditional steelpan, the tuning and instrument design are similar.

Instrument design and construction has been refined over time and is still evolving. Almost all handpans are constructed largely by hand and put into tune using a series of precise hammer blows. The handpan builder is able to tune the notes on the instrument to a range of different pitches, thus creating a wide variety of scales. The information, techniques, and theory presented in this book are designed to be flexible, and can be adapted to work on your instrument, no matter the scale or number of notes.

This book is written for a broad range of skill levels. Beginners will find the introductory material and exercises necessary to develop their touch and technical skill, while the advanced player will find instructions on how to execute high-level techniques, create sophisticated sounds, and build complex patterns.

HANDPAN SOUND MODELS (BASIC)

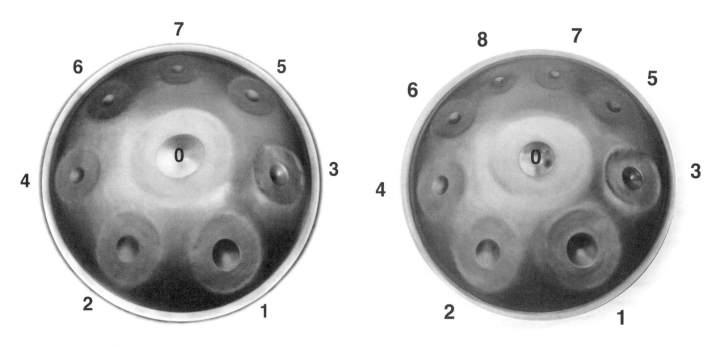

Fig. 1: Seven-Note Handpan   Fig. 2: Eight-Note Handpan

BEFORE YOU BEGIN

Congratulations on beginning your journey into the world of the handpan! This book will help you develop skills in touch, dexterity, and musicality, while providing a canvas on which to begin exploring songwriting and improvisation on this one-of-a-kind instrument.

This text is presented in three distinct stages: 1) Discovery, 2) Development, and 3) Competency. These stages are designed to build on each other, introducing an increasingly refined set of skills.

STAGE 1: DISCOVERY

Take time to get to know your handpan rather than rushing through the exercises in the book. Don't be afraid to make mistakes, experiment, and listen to your musical intuition. Concentrate on creating sound and get comfortable playing your new handpan.

Learning objectives:

- Learn how to position yourself in relation to your instrument.

- Begin finding sounds on your instrument.

- Be able to play ascending and descending scales.

STAGE 2: DEVELOPMENT

Formalize your practice, begin to refine your touch, and become increasingly fluid as a player. Explore the world of the handpan, observe what other players are doing, and determine what you like about their various playing styles. Break these elements down and add them into your own musical toolkit. With increasing practice, you will be able to incorporate diverse playing styles.

Learning objectives:

- Explore more complex sounds.

- Develop complete rhythmic patterns.

- Experiment with "fills."

STAGE 3: COMPETENCY

Build fluency in the musical language of the handpan. Begin to communicate musically with other musicians and be able to realize your musical voice. The learning process never completely ends, but when you become a competent player, you have reached a milestone of independence in your musical journey.

Learning objectives:

- Master advanced playing techniques.

- Experiment with improvisation.

- Build structured songs.

- Develop your own voice and style.

Good luck on the beginning of your musical adventure. Let this book help guide and inspire you to develop fresh ideas and unique approaches to the handpan. To help you along, terms in bold are defined in the glossary at the end of the book.

HANDPAN ANATOMY

A handpan is constructed of two bowl-shaped metal sheets fastened together in a spherical shape. The top of the handpan usually features seven, eight, or nine **tonefields** arranged in a circle around one **central note** (Fig. 3). The central note has a **dome** and at the center of each of the tonefields is a **dimple**. Notes along the outside of the instrument are arranged in a zig-zag orientation that ascends and descends in pitch following a natural alternating pattern of the hands.

Handpans are most often classified by the number of tonefields arranged in the outer circle (**tonecircle**), excluding the central note. Every handpan has a central note, regardless of the number of notes in its tonecircle. Therefore, instruments with eight total notes are referred to as seven-note instruments. Some custom instruments are built to accommodate more than nine notes and can occasionally have notes on the bottom as well.

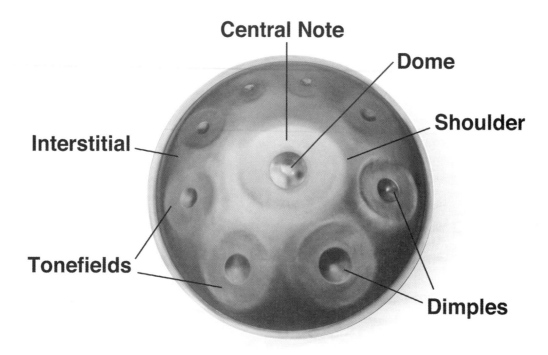

Fig. 3: Top

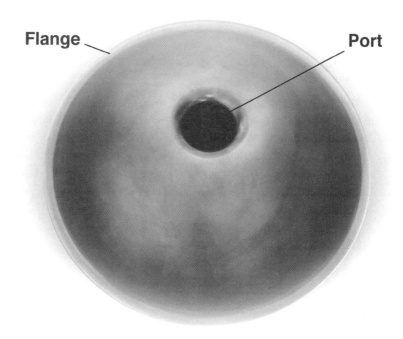

Fig. 4: Bottom

Each tonefield has a complex double-curve shape that conveys the unique tonal qualities of the instrument. Below is a 3D rendering of a tonefield (Figs. 5 & 6).

The shape of the note and the stiffness of the steel creates frequencies that are audible when the note rings. Alignment among the frequencies produces a good-sounding note. Most handpan notes are built to resonate with a fundamental tone, an octave harmonic, and a compound fifth harmonic. The frequencies that ring from each note and their subsequent interactions is what gives the handpan the rich and chorus-like sound that is so enjoyable. (See **sympathetic resonance**.)

Handpans are open resonant chambers. The bottom contains a port that allows sound to resonate (Fig. 4). This port can also be played to create deep percussive bass tones. (See **cavity resonance**.)

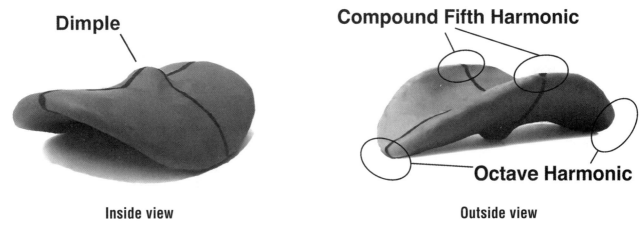

Dimple

Compound Fifth Harmonic

Octave Harmonic

Inside view

Fig. 5: Handpan note construction

Outside view

Fig. 6: Handpan note construction

Handpan scales are usually partial expressions of a common key, scale, or mode. Since there is no single standard model, the notes on a handpan can vary from instrument to instrument.

TIPS AND MAINTENANCE

- The steel of some handpans is specially heat-treated to make the instruments resistant to corrosion, but environmental conditions still affect the propensity for the instrument to rust. Keep your instrument clean, dry, and avoid storing it in humid conditions.

- Always ask the builder of your instrument how best to care for your instrument. All instruments are different and may need different maintenance and care.

- It is best not to store your instrument in its case for extended periods. If you must do so, you should facilitate airflow by unzipping the case and reduce moisture by adding a packet of desiccant.

- Play your instrument with care. Avoid heavy-handed strikes and never play with sticks, mallets, or other percussion accessories; such things may change the tensions in the steel and compromise the tuning.

- A well-built instrument should stay in tune for several years or longer. Re-tuning of an instrument should be done only by a professional, and by the original builder whenever possible.

- Avoid temperature extremes; direct sunlight may temporarily distort the instrument's tuning as the heat acts on the material.

READING THE TABLATURE

The following system is the result of a mixture of rhythmic-based tablature standards, which have been adapted for the particular complexities of the handpan. Notes are designated by numbers ascending from lowest to highest pitch (Fig. 1). The central, lowest note is always designated as zero (0) with the notes of the tonecircle ascending upward from one (1). The pitches of these numbers vary from handpan to handpan with different **tunings**.

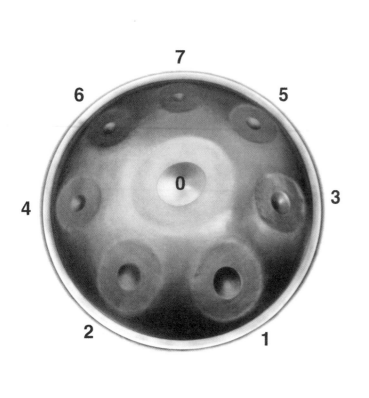

Fig. 1: Instrument notation

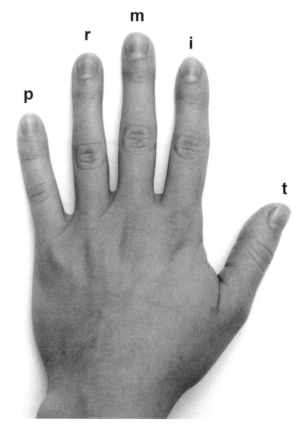

Fig. 7: Digit notation

STICKING AND FINGERING

The letters L and R are written below the tab lines indicating a left- or right-hand strike.

Characters t, i, m, r, and p placed below the tab indicate the specific finger used to play each note.

- t – Thumb

- i – Index

- m – Middle

- r – Ring

- p – Pinky

When absent, the choice of sticking and/or fingering is left to the player's discretion.

SPECIAL CHARACTERS

- Sounds like taks, interstitial clicks, fist strokes, etc. are indicated with special characters on the staff in place of the note number. These are discussed in detail as they are introduced later in the book.

- Articulations and other musical markings are contained above or on the staff as with any other standard notation.

RHYTHM

- The lines found above the staff are broken rhythmic stems and indicate the rate of speed at which the notes are moving. Quarter notes, 8th notes, and any other note durations are indicated here in standard rhythmic notation.

ADAPTING EXERCISES FOR YOUR HANDPAN

- If your handpan has a larger number of notes than the tablature, your central note will still be zero (0), and you will not play the notes above the highest number in the notation.

- If your handpan has a smaller number of notes, you may have to skip over the notes that aren't present on your instrument. (This may involve slightly adapting the rhythm or structure of some exercises.)

Ascending and descending the handpan using the index fingers starting on the left hand at the rate of an 8th note:

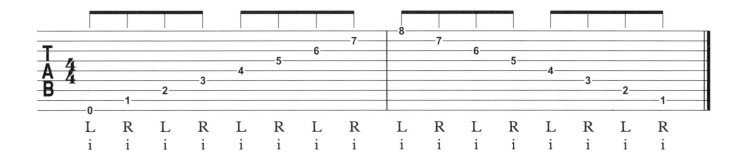

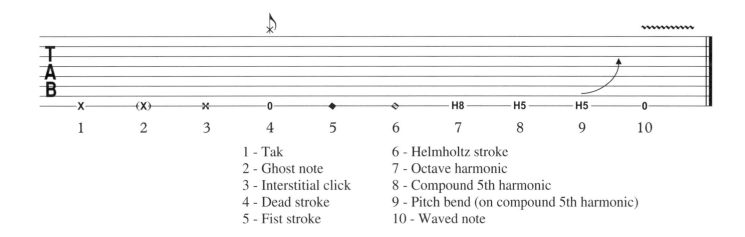

1 - Tak	6 - Helmholtz stroke
2 - Ghost note	7 - Octave harmonic
3 - Interstitial click	8 - Compound 5th harmonic
4 - Dead stroke	9 - Pitch bend (on compound 5th harmonic)
5 - Fist stroke	10 - Waved note

STAGE 1: DISCOVERY

- Learn how to position yourself in relation to your instrument.

- Begin finding sounds on your instrument.

- Be able to play ascending and descending scales.

PLAYING POSITIONS

Your handpan may be played in a variety of ways and positions. The best or most comfortable position will allow you to move around the instrument to access all the notes easily. Handpans come in different diameters and depths, so be prepared to try a few playing positions before settling on the one that works best for you. Many players position the largest tonefield (number one, see page 8) directly toward their stomach, this is a good place to begin.

Sitting

The handpan is most commonly played in a seated position. The legs are positioned in such a way that the instrument is tilted neither toward nor away from the player. If you have shorter legs, you can prop your feet up with a block to help keep the instrument in your lap (Fig. 10). It is also a good idea to experiment with chairs in a variety of heights. A handpan stand or snare drum stand with adjustable arms may be used to hold the instrument (Fig. 9). Make sure there are at least three points of contact, and that the contact surfaces are soft—preferably rubber. This will keep the surface from scratching. Some players prefer to sit on the floor, and, as with other playing positions, make sure you are comfortable and that all notes can be easily accessed (Fig. 11).

Fig. 9: Seated, using a stand

Fig. 10: Playing on the lap, feet supported by block

Fig. 11: Crossed-leg playing posture

Standing

Some players choose to stand in front of the handpan set on a stand (Fig. 12). Many players find that this position helps engage the whole body, enhancing their ability to move more fluidly around the instrument.

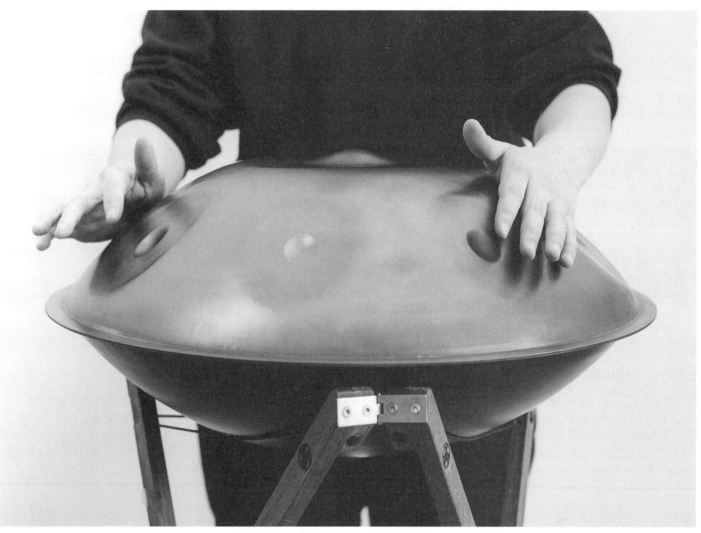

Fig. 12: Standing, using a stand

▶ DEVELOPING TOUCH

Tonefield sounds are produced by striking an area of the tonefield with the appropriate touch. Developing a touch is admittedly one of the most difficult things about playing the handpan for the first time, so it's important to be patient. Players often find success when first practicing a technique with the dominant hand, then allowing it to "teach" the non-dominant hand how to move.

Most strikes occur within the flattened tonefield; however, there is no single standard place to strike. You will come to discover that you can produce different timbres and overtones depending where on the **note body** (the entire region that includes the tonefield and the dimple) you connect.

The Basic Stroke

The basic stroke on the handpan is a complex gesture involving small and large muscle groups in the arm and hand; no single motion makes up the basic strike. In general, the louder the sound, the more muscle groups that will be used. Softer sounds require smaller and fewer muscle groups. The motion of the basic stroke is best visualized as a wave, beginning at your shoulder and ending at the tip of your finger.

First, practice the basic stroke without your handpan by moving your hand in the air in front of you in a whipping or wave-like motion that begins in your shoulder. Start at first with large movements and slowly progress to smaller movements. You should naturally feel your shoulder and elbow motions begin to move less and less as the motion gets smaller and your wrist and finger take a more leading role. This is the range of motion of dynamic playing. This basic stroke can be divided into two slight variations: striking with one of the four fingers or striking with the thumb.

Striking with the Finger

Beginning with the center note, strike the note body with one of the four fingers. This motion begins as a basic wave and ends with the wrist moving the hand directly up and down as if knocking on a flat surface. This vertical motion of the wrist and hand should transfer to the finger, which moves vertically as well.

It is important that the entire hand be capable of producing a high-quality sound. Developing strength and independence of touch in every finger will help achieve this. Use your index, middle, ring, or pinky finger to practice, following the same path of motion for every digit. The motion is the same as striking the center note, but the vertical motion is translated slightly to strike at an angle perpendicular to the note plane (Figs. 13, 14 & 15). Practice sound quality and control using slow, repeated strikes at a constant tempo. Explore how slight alterations in your strike create different sounds and timbres.

 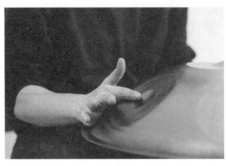 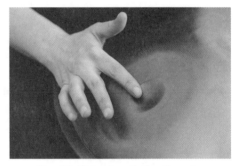

Fig. 13: Upward stroke (index finger)　　Fig. 14: Downward stroke (index finger)　　Fig. 15: Side view (index finger)

Striking with the Thumb

Striking the instrument with the thumb requires a slightly different set of motions relative to striking the central note with your fingers. Start with the basic wave motion, but translate the vertical motion with a rotation of the wrist, as if turning a door knob (Fig. 16). At the bottom of the stroke where the thumb is in contact with the handpan (Fig. 17 & 18), your palm should be facing downward, after which the wrist rotates to turn the palm perpendicular to the floor as the elbow and remainder of the arm lift the hand from the instrument surface. This motion should be fluid.

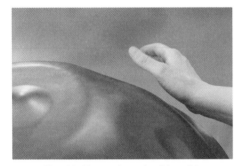  

Fig. 16: Upward stroke (thumb)　　Fig. 17: Downward stroke (thumb)　　Fig. 18: Side view (thumb)

Refining the Strike

To create a full-sounding resonant strike that has little attack sound, strike where the dimple meets the flat area of the note body. Connect with the fleshiest, most padded part of the striking digit at a 45-degree angle. Striking this way will create the smallest amount of skin-to-metal contact and will result in a warm, rounded sound.

It helps to visualize the motion as not playing "on" the instrument, but "pulling" the sound out. Implement the flowing wave motion and allow the finger to lift gently from the tonefield surface, pulling the sound out with it. The strike must be quick yet very relaxed. Remember: every muscle is engaged in this process from shoulder, to elbow, to wrist, to finger. Practice sound quality and control using slow, repeated strikes at a constant tempo.

TOUCH DEVELOPMENT EXERCISES

Exercise 1.1 includes a crescendo (gradual volume increase) and decrescendo (gradual volume decrease), indicated by the lines underneath the figure.

Handpans are naturally soft-spoken instruments, so you may want to increase the intensity of your stroke to produce a louder sound. Don't! The key to extracting more volume from your instrument comes from playing with technique that lets the instrument resonate to its fullest ability. Only then can you begin to increase the intensity of your stroke. In short, playing a poor-quality sound harder will not create a good quality sound; instead, this is one of the easiest and most common ways instruments are damaged.

For Exercise 1.1, strike any note with your dominant hand, then play it with your opposite hand when you feel ready. Next, play with both hands on separate notes (pick any notes for now); strike the notes simultaneously at first.

Exercise 1.1

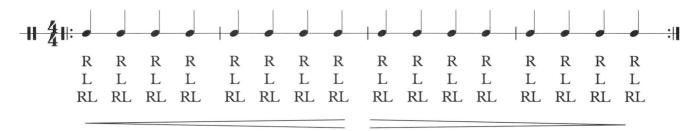

Focus on building touch proficiency with all digits; this is the foundation to more advanced techniques. Be sure to avoid hard strikes directly on joints or bones, especially on the thumb. Developing good technique is challenging, but it is better to take it slow than cause discomfort or injury.

Exploring the range of the instrument is the next step. Maintain the integrity of the basic stroke while ascending and descending the notes of the handpan in an alternating (zig-zag) pattern. Keep repeating the exercise and cycle through every finger on your hand. Your goal should be to maintain a sound that is consistent and indistinguishable from finger to finger. Repeat each bar as many times as necessary and keep a steady 8th-note rhythm throughout.

Exercise 1.2

Seven-Note Handpan

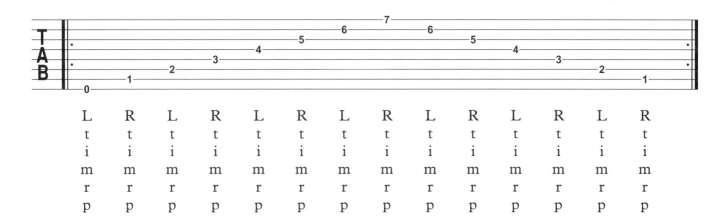

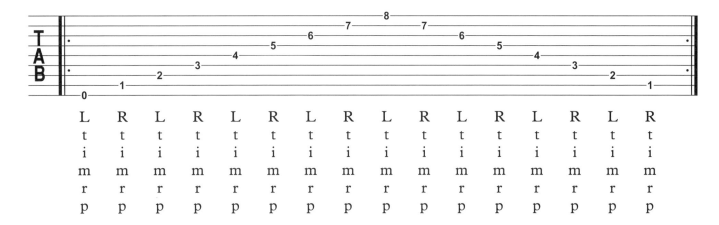

Rotate the handpan 180 degrees so that the highest note is now closest to your body. You will notice that the position of the notes has changed, requiring you to adjust your aim slightly to achieve a high-quality sound. Do not change your strike or fingering pattern. The only difference is that the handpan is oriented with the highest note closest to your body. Rotating the instrument like this can be done for any exercise or pattern in this book and can be a great way to create a fresh approach.

Exercise 1.3

Seven-Note Handpan

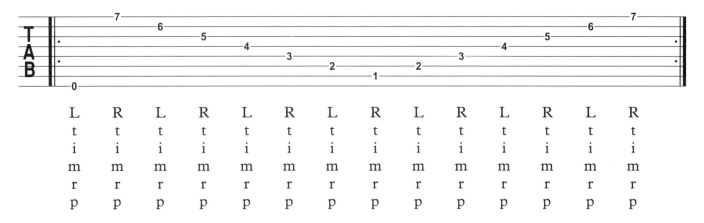

Eight-Note Handpan

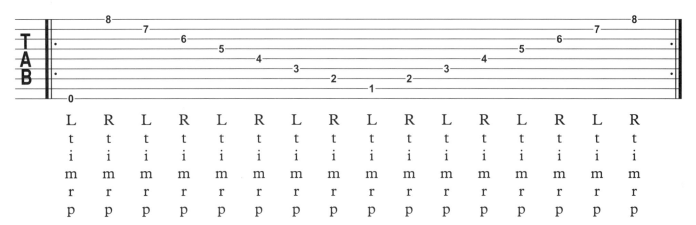

Beginning players often want to confine their right and left hands to the right and left sides of the instrument, but practicing crossing the instrument will improve your ability to play fluidly. When crossing the instrument, it is important to keep the hands low to the surface to minimize the distance traveled from note to note. Your hands may touch the instrument and create ambient noise; this is not necessarily wrong and is a natural part of playing the handpan. Practice this technique by repeating Exercise 1.2, but this time using only one hand at a time.

Exercise 1.4

Seven-Note Handpan

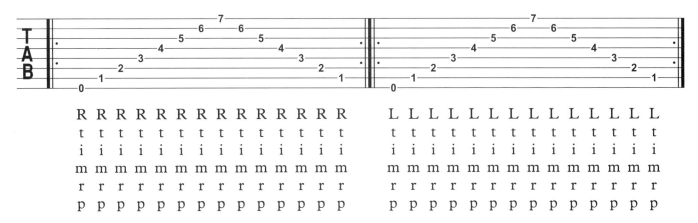

Eight-Note Handpan

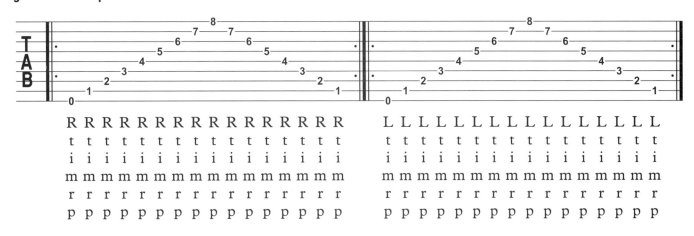

Repeat the exercise a third time, but this time alternate the hands and play a steady 16th-note rhythm throughout. By superimposing both hands' parts over each other, we have a new and challenging exercise.

Exercise 1.5

Seven-Note Handpan

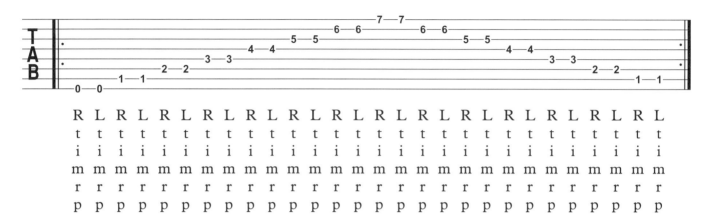

```
R L R L R L R L R L R L R L R L R L R L R L R L R L R L R L R L R L
t   t   t   t   t   t   t   t   t   t   t   t   t   t   t   t
i   i   i   i   i   i   i   i   i   i   i   i   i   i   i   i
m m m m m m m m m m m m m m m m m m m m m m m m m m m m m m m m
r   r   r   r   r   r   r   r   r   r   r   r   r   r   r   r
p p p p p p p p p p p p p p p p p p p p p p p p p p p p p p p p
```

Eight-Note Handpan

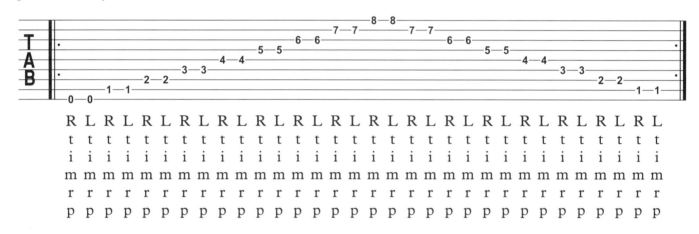

```
R L R L R L R L R L R L R L R L R L R L R L R L R L R L R L R L R L
t   t   t   t   t   t   t   t   t   t   t   t   t   t   t   t
i   i   i   i   i   i   i   i   i   i   i   i   i   i   i   i
m m m m m m m m m m m m m m m m m m m m m m m m m m m m m m m m
r   r   r   r   r   r   r   r   r   r   r   r   r   r   r   r
p p p p p p p p p p p p p p p p p p p p p p p p p p p p p p p p
```

TWO-NOTE STROKES

Playing two neighboring notes at the same time using a single hand will greatly expand harmonic possibilities. Begin by placing your hand into an open position, creating an L-shape with your thumb and either the index finger, middle finger, or ring finger (Fig. 19). Two-note strokes use a motion that is somewhere between the rotation motion used for the thumb strike and the wrist-bend motion used for the finger strike. Strike the instrument with both fingers, following the principles of the basic stroke. As your hands move to different parts of the instrument, the balance of wrist rotation and wrist break will change. Each finger should connect with the metal at the same time.

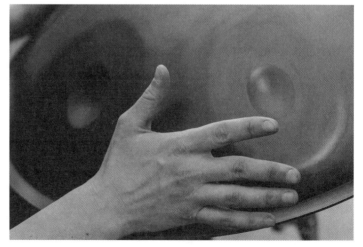

Fig. 19: L-shape of hand, two-note strokes

To practice this, revisit Exercise 1.1, but this time add two notes to a single hand. Here the exercise includes bar lines and quarter-note rhythms.

Exercise 1.6

Seven- and Eight-Note Handpan

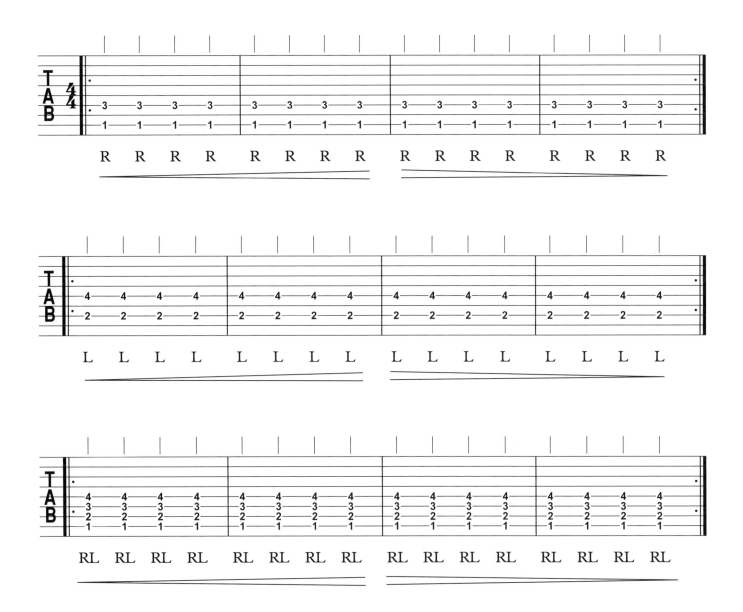

Move around the instrument using two-note strokes. As your arms extend away from your body, you will discover that you need to rotate your wrist more than you bend it. As your arms retract, you will bend your wrist more than it rotates. Practice this motion in Exercise 1.7. You can experiment with any finger and thumb combination (ti, tm, tr) that works best for you on your instrument.

Exercise 1.7

Seven-Note Handpan

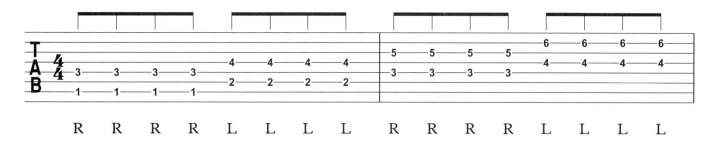

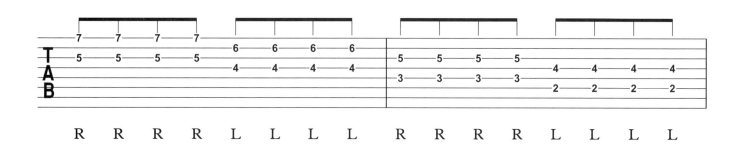

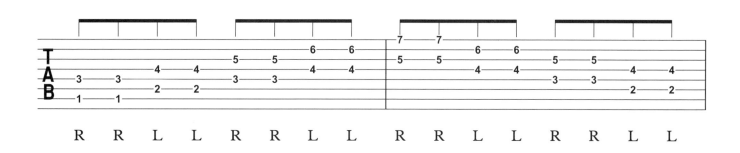

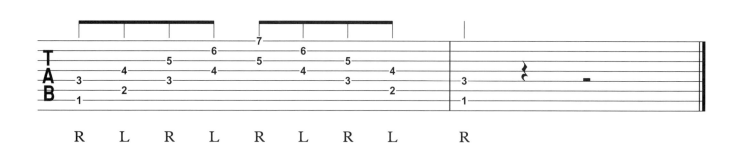

Eight-Note Handpan

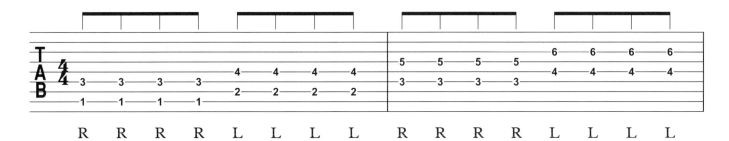

R R R R L L L L R R R R L L L L

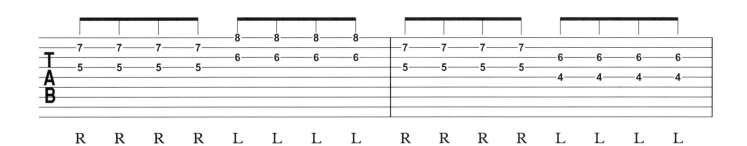

R R R R L L L L R R R R L L L L

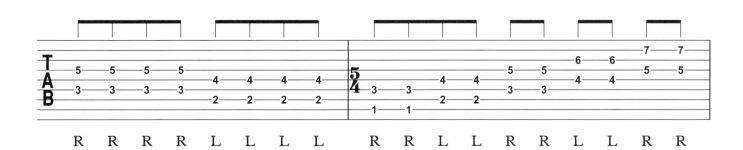

R R R R L L L L R R L L R R L L R R

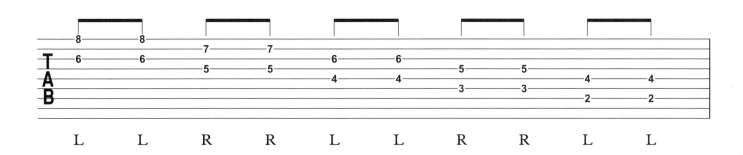

L L R R L L R R L L

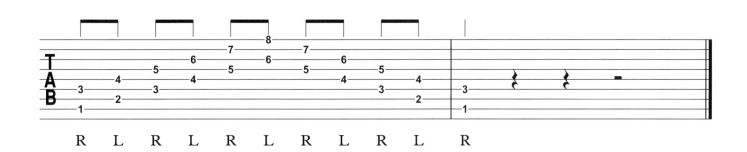

R L R L R L R L R L R

PLAYING CHORDS

Using two-note strokes, you can begin to build larger harmonic groupings called "chords." Due to the natural alternating layout of the handpan, chords are often formed by neighboring notes. By combining one-note and two-note strokes, you can create three-note chords. Simultaneous two-note strokes using both hands create chords of up to four notes.

Adding the central note is an easy way to expand harmonies. Here, the central note is added to the pattern from Exercise 1.7.

Exercise 1.8

Seven-Note Handpan

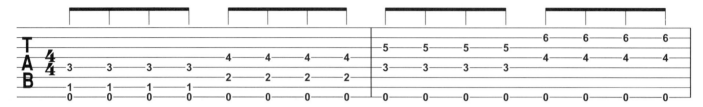

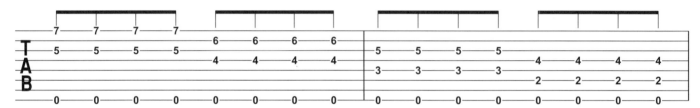

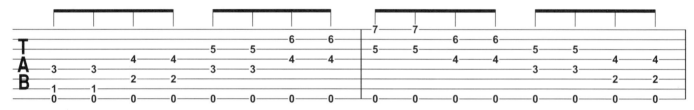

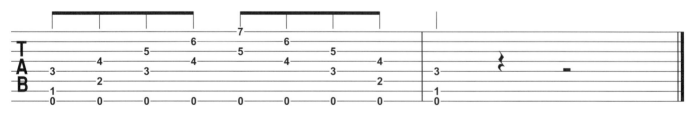

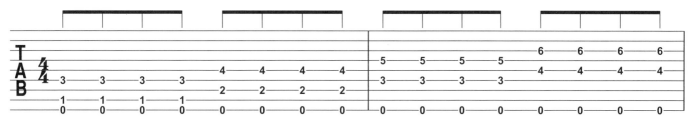

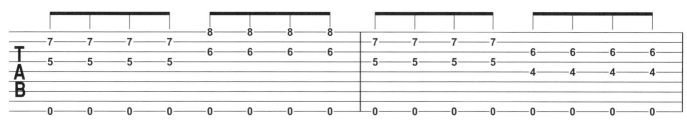

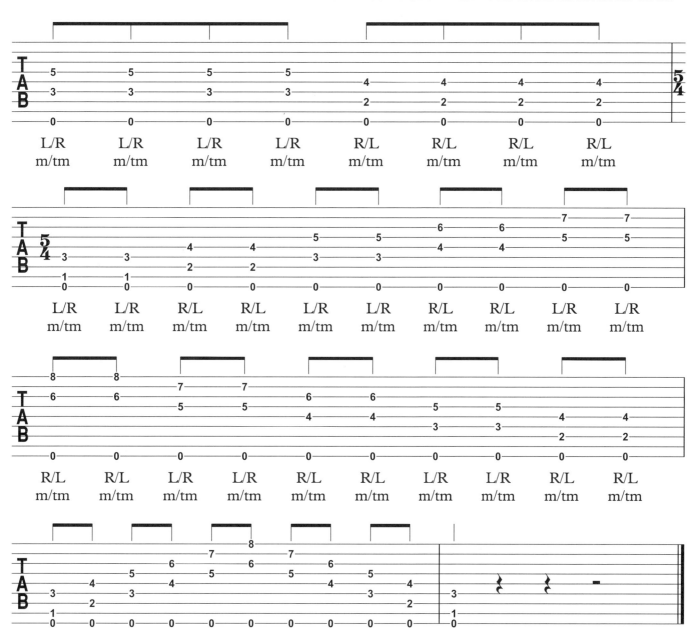

Practice moving from three-note chord to three-note chord, ascending and descending in pitch.

Exercise 1.9

Seven-Note Handpan

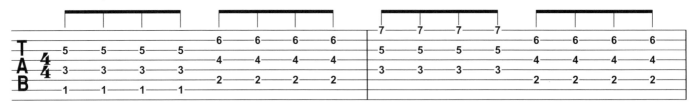

Eight-Note Handpan

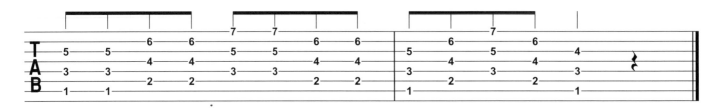

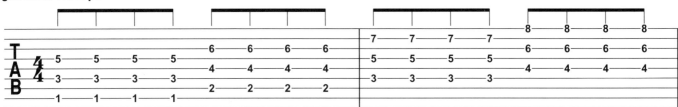

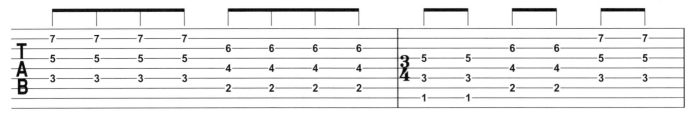

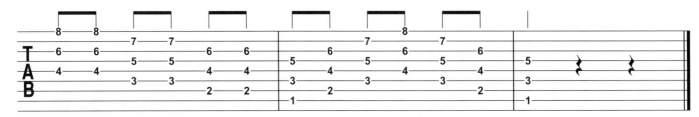

Chords can be broken apart into their constituent notes, forming arpeggios. Arpeggios may be used to add depth and rhythmic complexity to your playing. Exercise 1.10 repeats the chords presented in Exercise 1.9 as arpeggios.

Exercise 1.10

Seven-Note Handpan

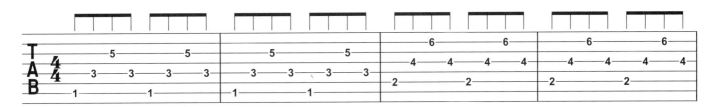

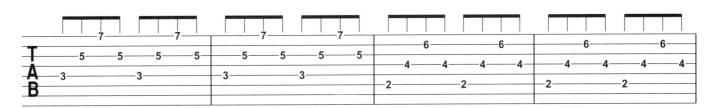

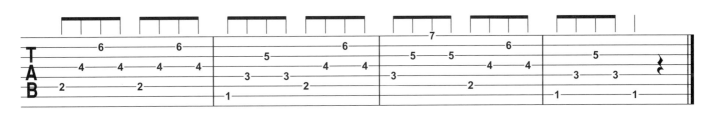

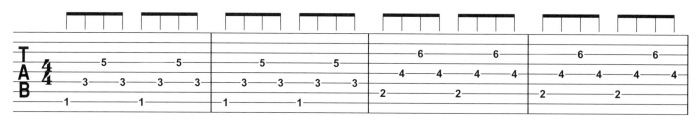

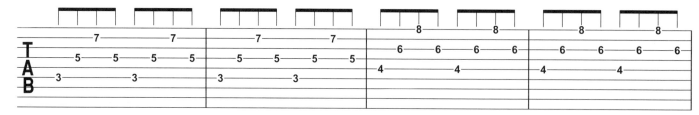

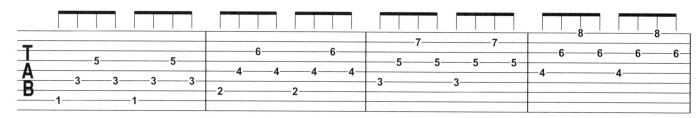

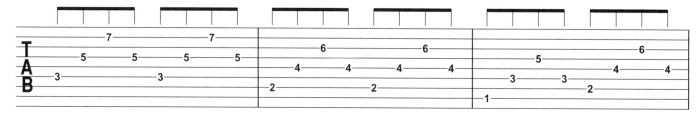

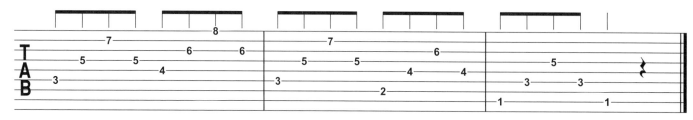

OTHER INTRODUCTORY TECHNIQUES

Introduction to Port Playing

Flip the instrument over and use the basic strike around the edges of the **port** to hear bell-like tones. You can also try flattening one hand and bringing it down over top of the port to draw out the instrument's low tones, or cavity resonance (Fig. 20). Experiment with the sounds. When mixed, the sounds can be a fantastic percussive accompaniment to a variety of other instruments that may not be playing in the same scale or key as your handpan.

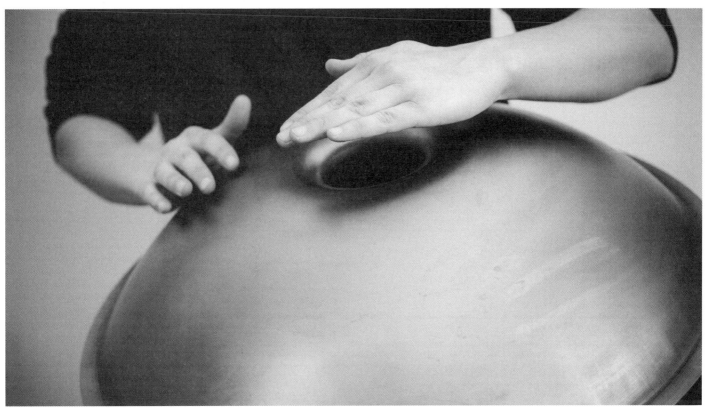

Fig. 20: Activating the cavity resonance on the port side

Fig. 21: Vertical playing position

Introduction to Vertical Playing

By tilting the instrument vertically in your lap, you can access both the portside and the topside (Fig. 21). This is useful for setting a rhythm on the port while adding one-handed melody on the top shell of the instrument.

♩ = 80

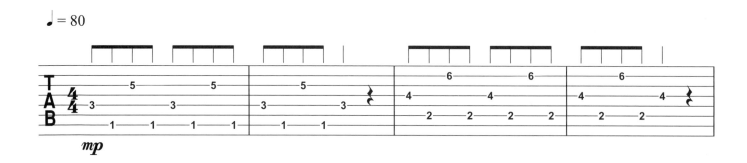

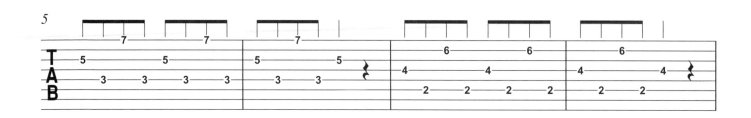

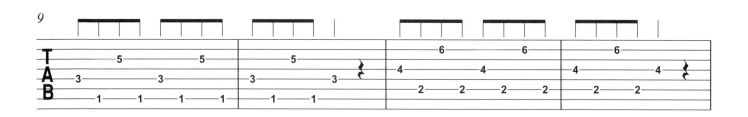

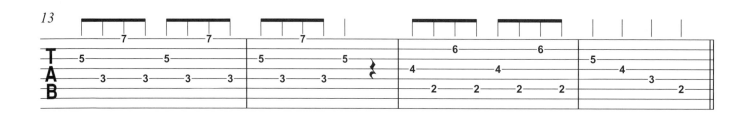

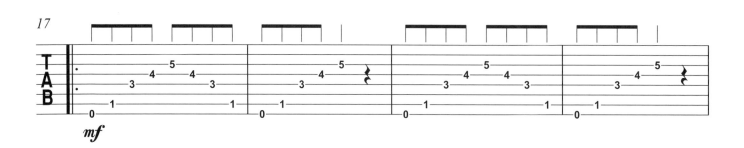

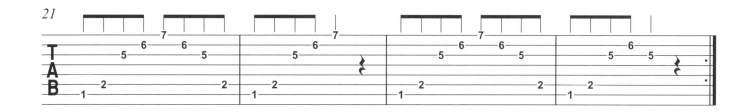

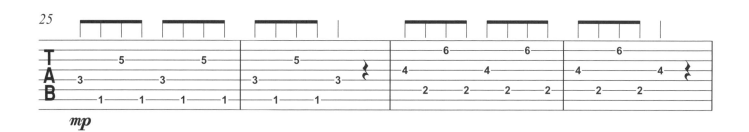

mp

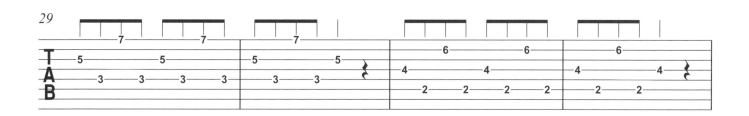

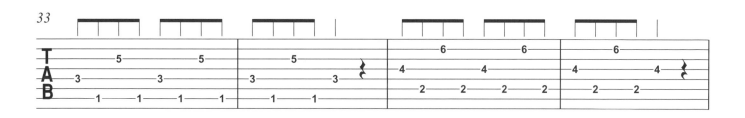

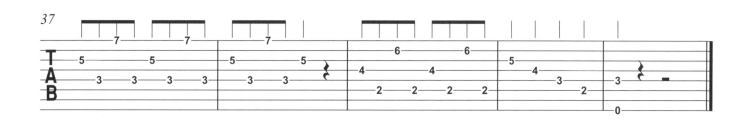

▶ EIGHT-NOTE HANDPAN ETUDE NO. 1

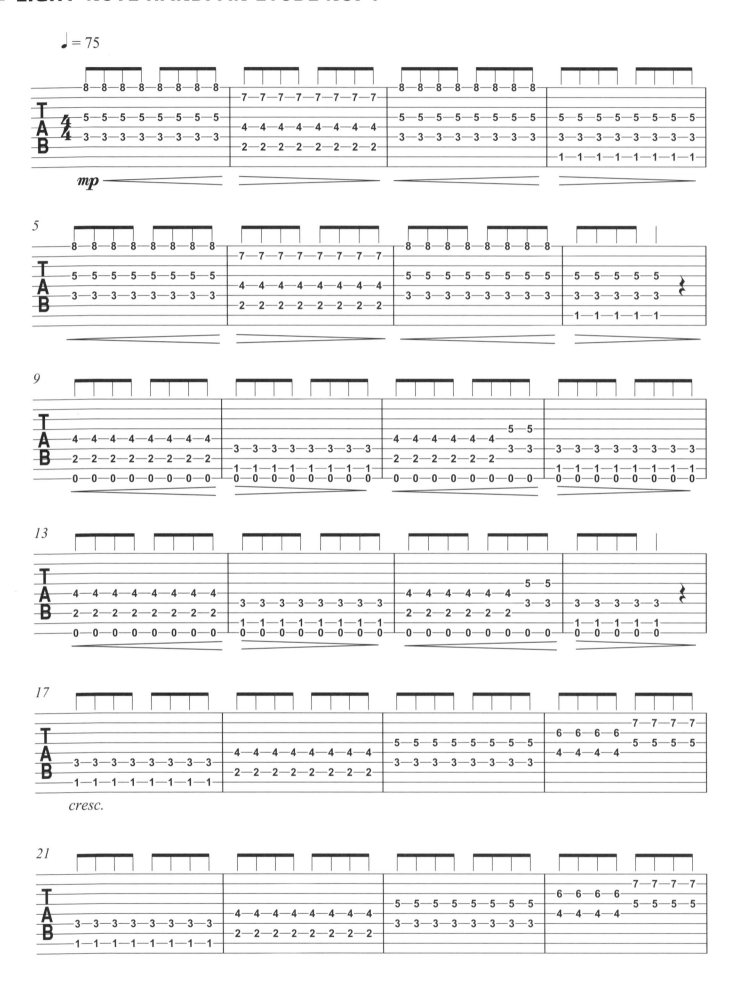

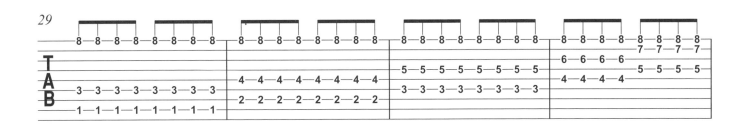

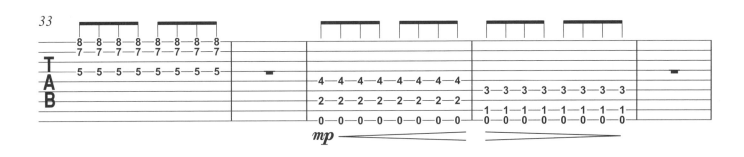

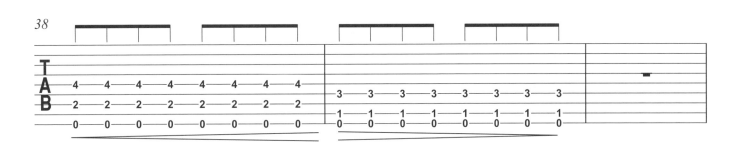

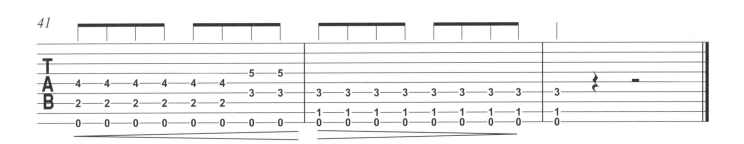

STAGE 2: DEVELOPMENT

- Explore more complex sounds.

- Develop complete rhythmic patterns.

- Experiment with "fills."

PERCUSSIVE SOUNDS

The handpan's ability to create both percussive and melodic sounds is one of its most fascinating characteristics. The next section introduces a few of the most popular percussive sounds that can be used in various combinations.

▶ The Tak

The **tak** is a high-pitched percussive sound played near the shoulder (outer edge) of the central note (Figs. 22 & 23). The tak can be viewed as a combination of two separate sounds: 1) the dull ceramic clicking sound that comes from the interstitial space between the central note's shoulder and the surrounding tonefields; 2) the lively ringing sound of the flat part of the area surrounding the dome of the central note. To achieve a sharp, crisp-sounding tak, split the difference between the two zones, striking the very edge of the shoulder with your finger, connecting at a 45-degree angle. If the tak sounds dead, try moving your finger closer to the flat of the shoulder. If it is too wild, try pulling back to connect more with the interstitial space. Taks are great to fill empty space in a groove and can add color to simple ideas. The tak is designated with an "x" in the exercises that follow.

Fig. 22: The tak area, near the shoulder of the central note

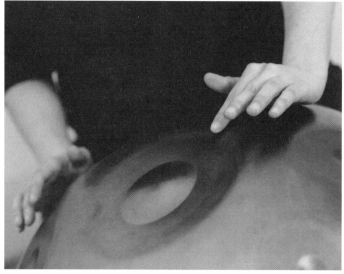
Fig. 23: Playing the tak sound

Ghost Notes

A **ghost note** is a stroke played at a very low volume; it is used to fill out a groove and maintain a sense of rhythm among other notes. Ghost notes are marked in parentheses.

▶ Interstitial Clicks

The sharpest, loudest, and most distinguishable percussive sound comes from the **interstitial click**. The interstitial area of the handpan is the untuned area on the top of a shell between and around the tonefields. To execute the interstitial click, strike a smooth area of the handpan well outside any tonefield with a fast movement of the finger that remains on the surface of the metal after initial contact. This is commonly referred to as a dead stroke. For the loudest sound, aim to connect the finger to the steel at the third knuckle of either your index or middle finger. The resulting sound should be crisp, snappy, and ceramic-like. Interstitial clicks may be played similarly to how a drummer uses a snare drum, or how you might clap along to a song. Interstitial clicks are notated by a bold "**x**."

CREATING A GROOVE

Because of its large array of sounds, the central note makes an ideal starting point for developing a rhythmic base. Use the basic central note stroke as a bass voice, taks to keep the rhythm, and eventually add in interstitial clicks or any other sounds for punctuation. This set of sounds can be used similarly to the bass drum, hi-hat, and snare drum of a drumset, or the various strokes of a darbuka, cajón, djembe, or other percussion. Below are a few basic exercises to develop coordination and the ability to switch among various sounds.

Exercise 2.1

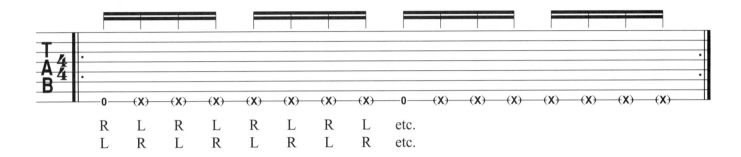

Note: Make sure the central note is resonating fully and try to keep the ghost notes at a low volume; they are here just to fill out the groove. Begin with your dominant hand and repeat as many times as necessary, then try leading with your non-dominant hand.

Now make the groove more interesting by adding accents (emphasis) to the taks on beats two and four.

Exercise 2.2

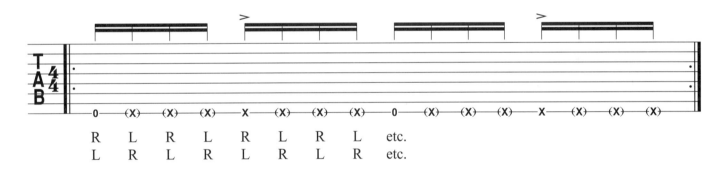

Develop Exercise 2.2 one step further by replacing the accented taks with interstitial clicks on beats two and four.

Exercise 2.3

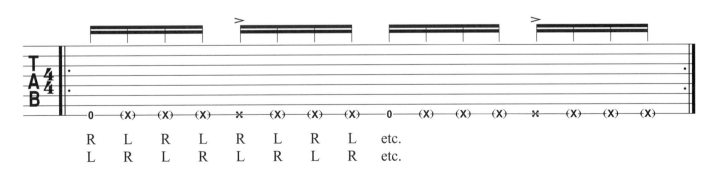

From here, begin to move different sounds to different parts of the beat to create new patterns. For new inspiration, experiment with adapting grooves from other percussion instruments to your handpan. Here are a few to get you started.

Exercise 2.4 – Rock groove #1

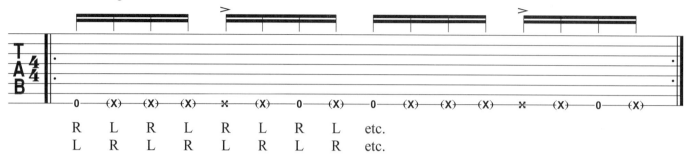

```
R   L   R   L   R   L   R   L   etc.
L   R   L   R   L   R   L   R   etc.
```

Exercise 2.5 – Rock groove #2

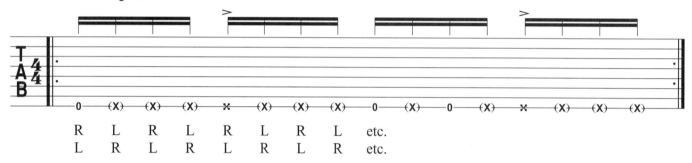

```
R   L   R   L   R   L   R   L   etc.
L   R   L   R   L   R   L   R   etc.
```

Exercise 2.6 – Funk groove #1

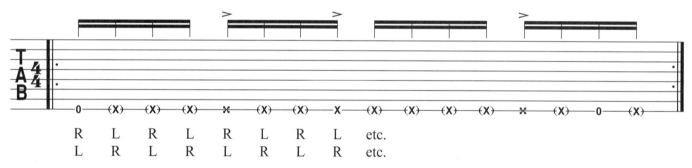

```
R   L   R   L   R   L   R   L   etc.
L   R   L   R   L   R   L   R   etc.
```

Exercise 2.7 – Funk groove #2

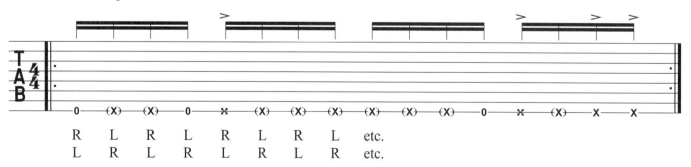

```
R   L   R   L   R   L   R   L   etc.
L   R   L   R   L   R   L   R   etc.
```

The following exercises are two-voice traditional rhythmic patterns. Experiment with these, using a combination of any two distinct sounds on your handpan.

Exercise 2.8 – Bossa Nova

Exercise 2.9 – Samba

Exercise 2.10 – Malfuf

Exercise 2.11 – Maqsoum

FILLS

A **fill** is short melodic or rhythmic variation in a pattern. Fills are used in a transition or at the end of a phrase (group of repeated patterns). Fills can add variation to playing, and are most commonly used in drumset playing. Try pairing different grooves from Exercises 2.1–2.11 with these different fills to make new and exciting combinations.

Exercise 2.12 – Fills, moving up the scale

Seven-Note Handpan

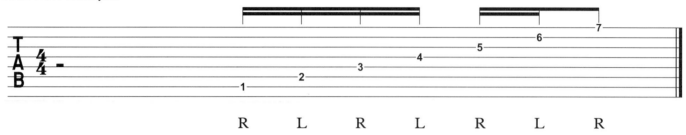

Eight-Note Handpan

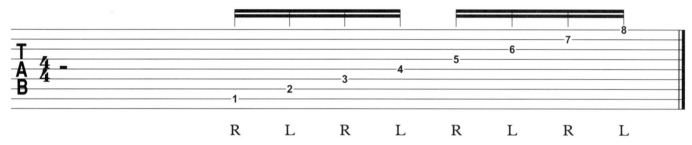

Exercise 2.13 – Fills, moving down the scale

Seven-Note Handpan

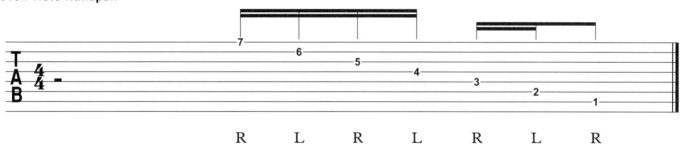

Eight-Note Handpan

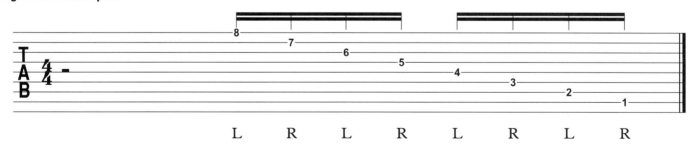

Exercise 2.14 – Fills, moving up and down the scale

Seven-Note Handpan

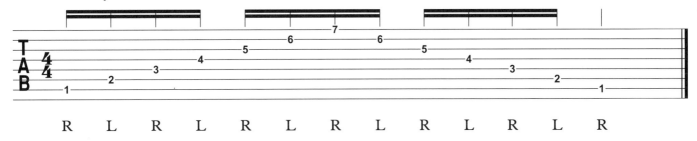

R L R L R L R L R L R L R

Eight-Note Handpan

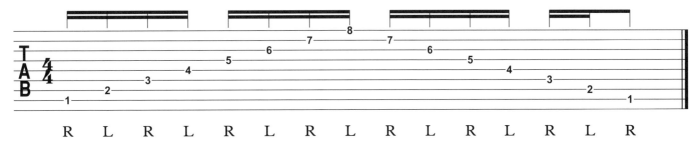

R L R L R L R L R L R L R L R

Exercise 2.15 – Fills, moving up by groupings of 3

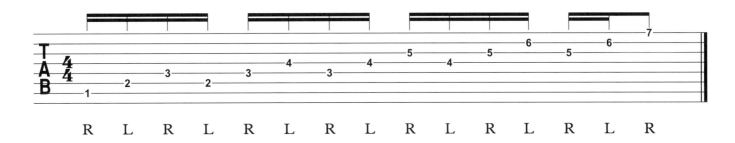

R L R L R L R L R L R L R L R

Exercise 2.16 – Fills, moving down by groupings of 3

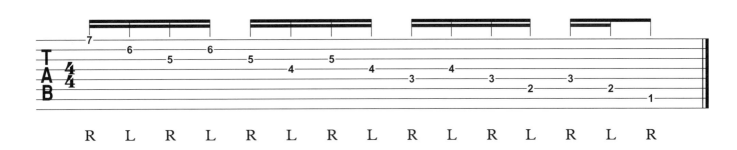

R L R L R L R L R L R L R L R

Exercise 2.17 – Groups of 3 breakdown

Seven-Note Handpan

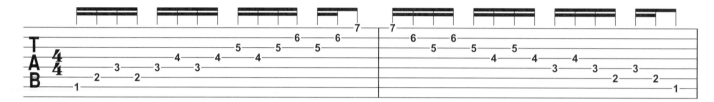

R L R L R L R L R L R L R L R   R L R L R L R L R L R L R L R

R L R L R L R L R L R L R L R   R L R L R L R L R L R L R L R

R L R L R L R L R L R L R L R L   R L R L R L R L R L R L R L R

Eight-Note Handpan

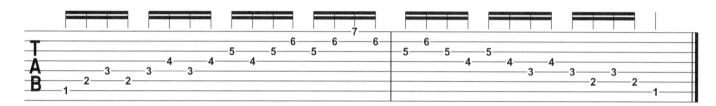

R L R L R L R L R L R L R L R L R L   L R L R L R L R L R L R L R L R L R

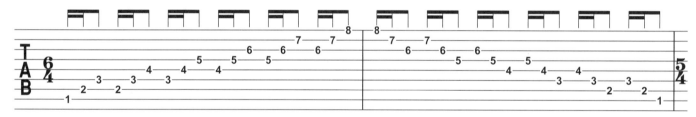

R L R L R L R L R L R L R L R L R L   L R L R L R L R L R L R L R L R L R

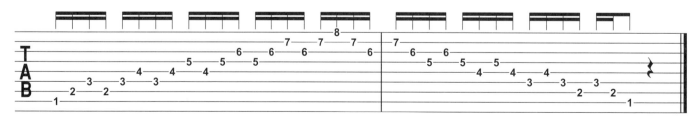

R L R L R L R L R L R L R L R L R L R L   R L R L R L R L R L R L R L R

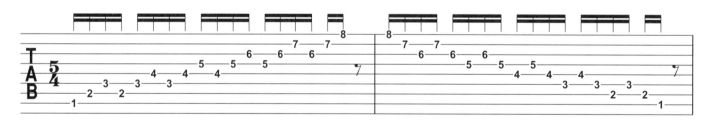

Exercise 2.18 – Fills, moving up by groupings of 4

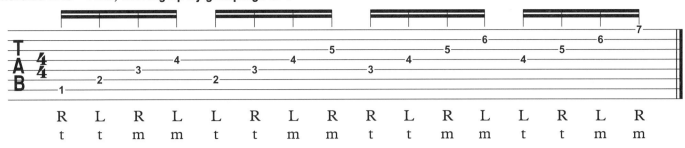

R L R L L R L R R L R L L R L R
t t m m t t m m t t m m t t m m

Exercise 2.19 – Fills, moving down by groupings of 4

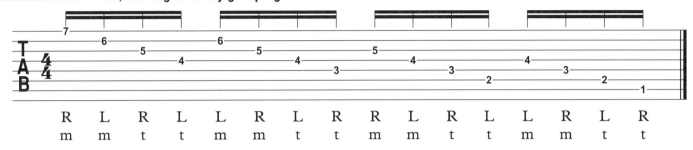

R L R L L R L R R L R L L R L R
m m t t m m t t m m t t m m t t

Exercise 2.20 – Groups of 4 breakdown

Seven-Note Handpan

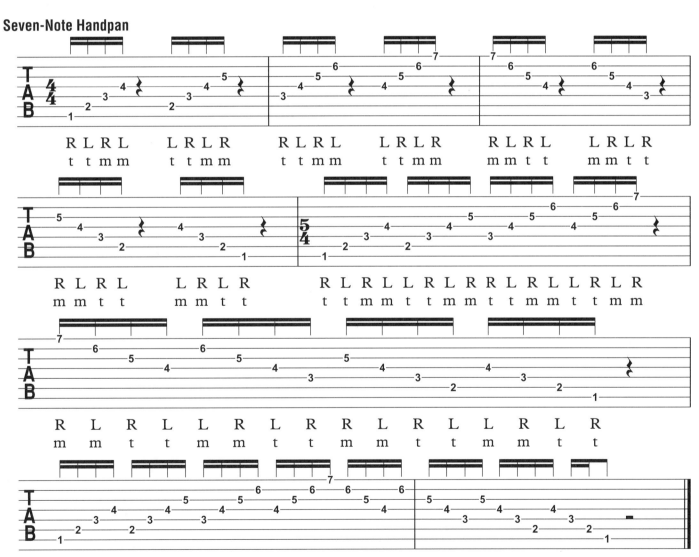

R L R L   L R L R   R L R L   L R L R   R L R L   L R L R
t t m m   t t m m   t t m m   t t m m   m m t t   m m t t

R L R L   L R L R   R L R L L R L R R L R L L R L R
m m t t   m m t t   t t m m t t m m t t m m t t m m

R L R L L R L R R L R L L R L R
m m t t m m t t m m t t m m t t

R L R L L L R L R R L R L L R L R L R L L   R L R R L R L L R L R
t t m m t t t m m t t m m t t m m m t t t m   m t t m m t t m m t t

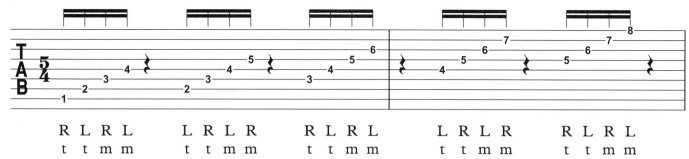

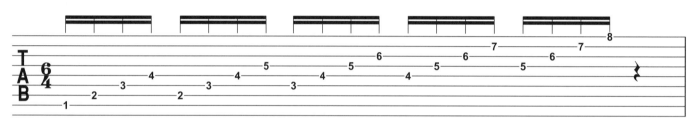

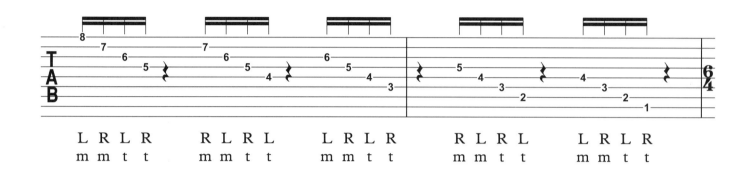

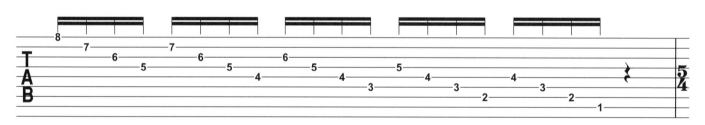

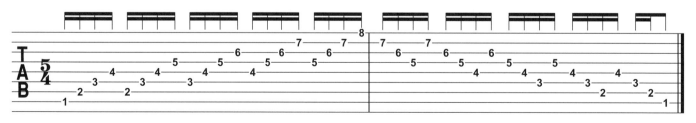

Exercise 2.21 – Fills, moving up by groupings of 5

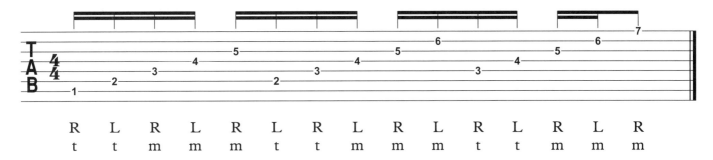

R L R L R L R L R L R L R L R L R
t t m m m t t m m m t t m m m

Exercise 2.22 – Fills, moving down by groupings of 5

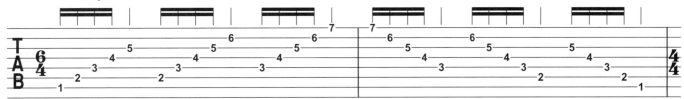

R L R L R L R L R L R L R L R
m m m t t m m m t t m m m t t

Exercise 2.23 – Groups of 5 breakdown

Seven-Note Handpan

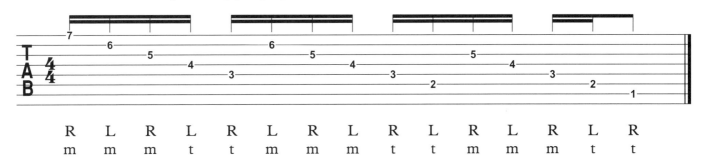

R L R L R   L R L R L   R L R L R   R L R L R   L R L R L   R L R L R
t t m m m   t t m m m   t t m m m   m m m t t   m m m t t   m m m t t

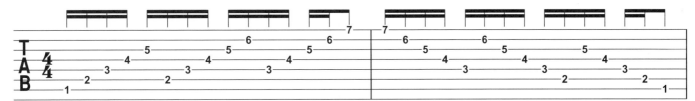

R L R L R L R L R L R L R L R   R L R L R L R L R L R L R L R
t t m m m t t m m m t t m m m   m m m t t m m m t t m m m t t

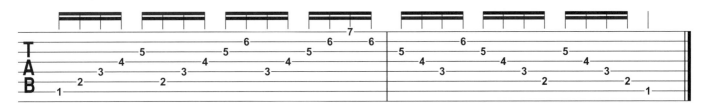

R L R L R L R L R L R L R L R L   R L R L R L R L R L R L R L R
t t m m m t t m m m t t m m m m   m t t m m m t t m m m t t

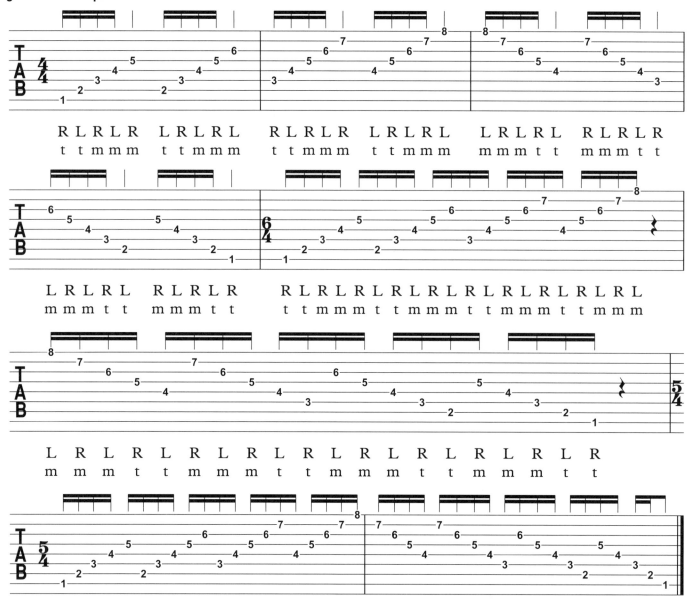

HAND COORDINATION

Continue to challenge your abilities with these developed coordination exercises.

Exercise 2.24 – Playing in 6/8

Seven-Note Handpan

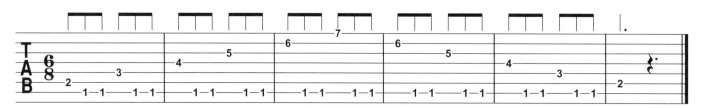

Eight-Note Handpan

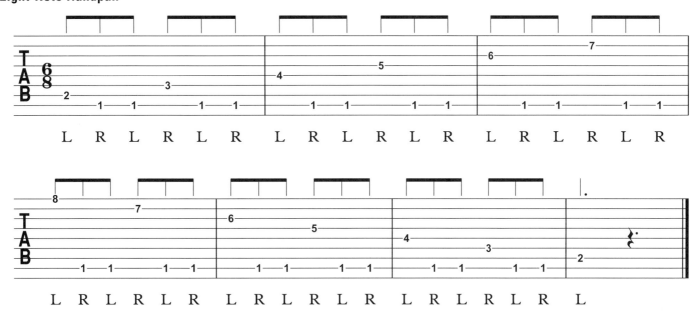

Exercise 2.25 – Hand Coordination

Seven-Note Handpan

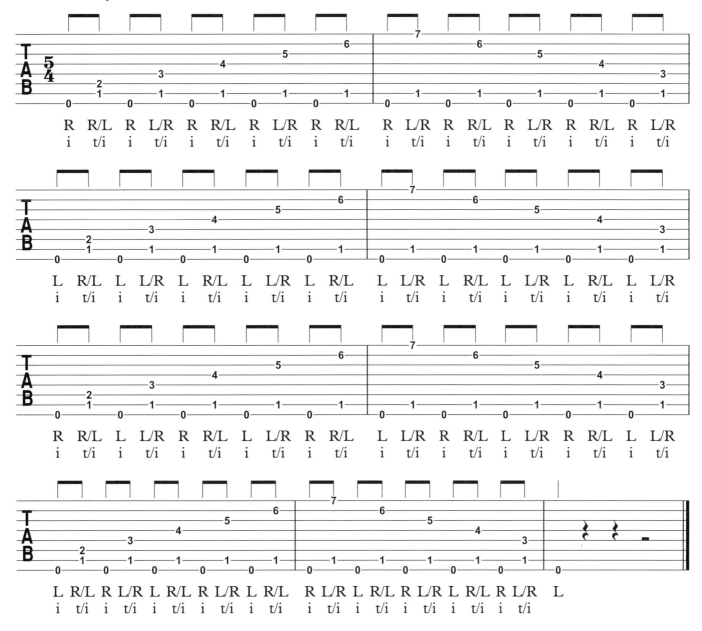

Eight-Note Handpan

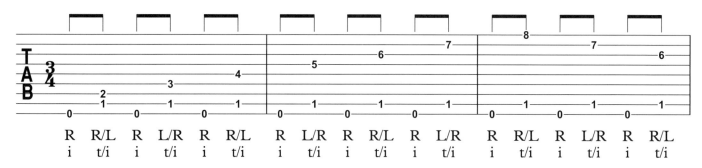

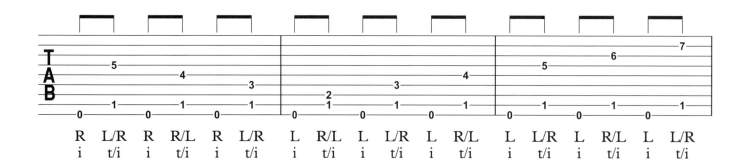

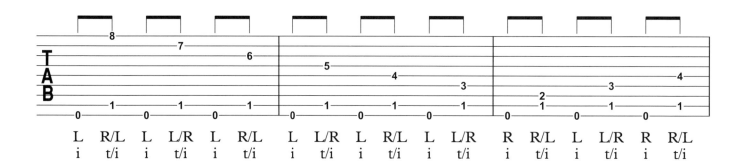

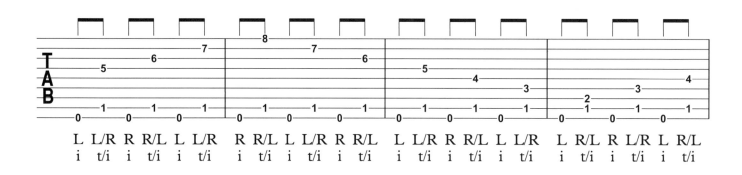

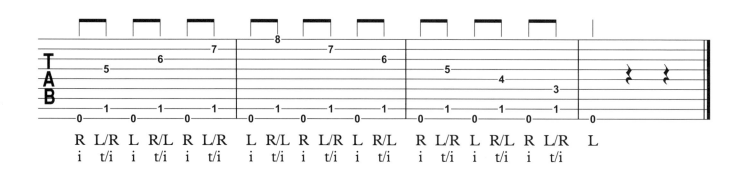

42

ROTATION STROKES

A rotation stroke creates two strikes with a single movement of the arm. To implement the rotation stroke on a handpan, start with two notes that neighbor each other. Position your hand in a check-mark shape similar to that of a two-note stroke. Strike with your thumb, then lift your hand from the elbow while rotating your thumb upward. Strike the second note with one of your fingers as you continue to rotate your wrist and lift your hand away from the instrument. You should hear two distinct strokes. It helps to relax: the second stroke should occur nearly involuntarily as a result of the rotation of your hand. You can perform rotation strokes starting with your thumb, or in reverse, starting with a finger followed by your thumb. Rotation strokes can effectively double your playing speed as you produce two tones with one motion. This technique can be used to arpeggiate chords, play scalar runs, grace notes, or even to add to grooves on the central note.

Exercise 2.26

Eight-Note Handpan

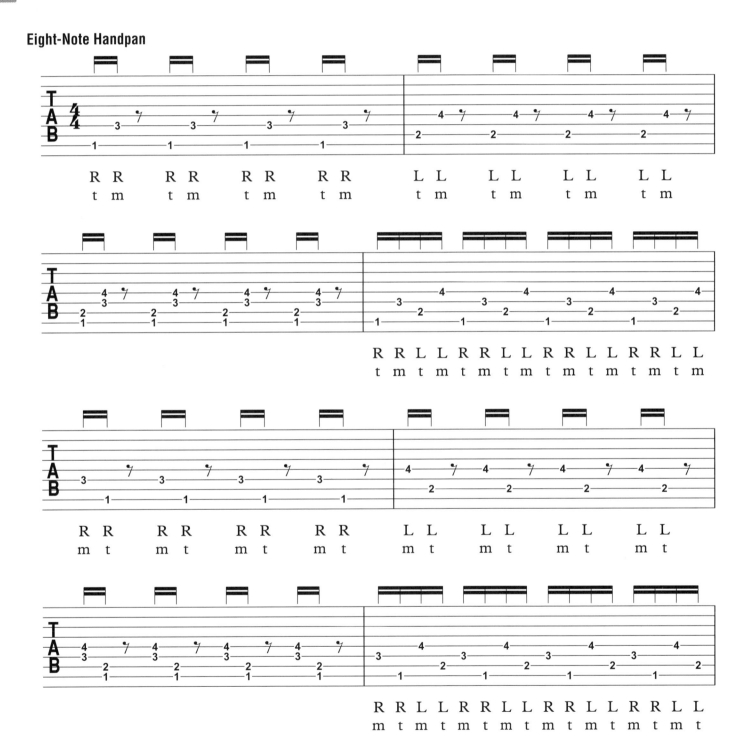

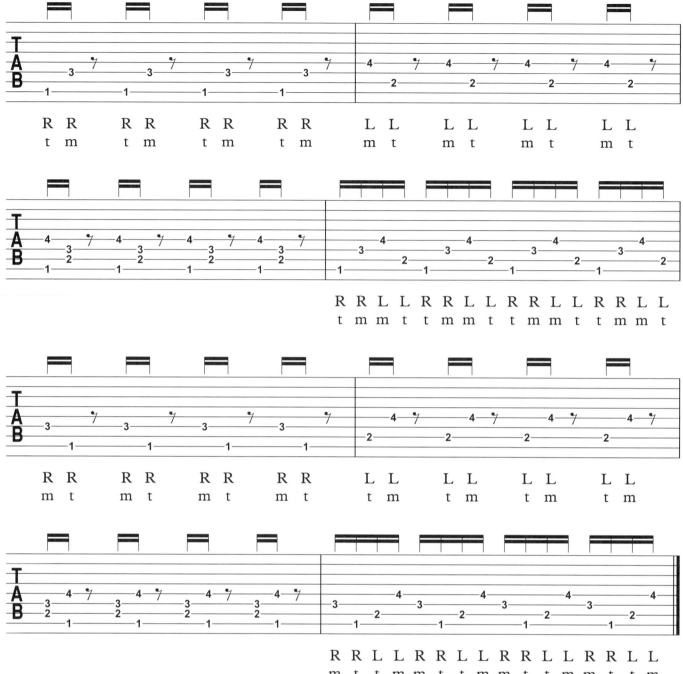

FLAMS

A **flam** is a percussive rudiment of two strokes in which the first stroke is kept at a low volume and shortly precedes the second stroke. This added first stroke can also be called a "grace note." It is important that the primary (second) stroke always lands directly on the beat and the grace note (first stroke) is placed just before the beat. The result is a sound that is thick, full, and textured. The amount of space between a grace note and a primary note is left up to the performer. Experiment with flams that are very open (much time between the grace note and primary stroke) and flams that are very closed (little time between the grace note and primary stroke). Experiment by adding flams into some of the previous fills.

INTERMEDIATE PLAYING TECHNIQUES

The following exercises and pictures will introduce more complex ways to create sound on your handpan.

▶ Dead Strokes

To add variation to your playing, try striking a note and letting your hand rest on the metal surface rather than rebounding off. Do this gently, making sure not to add any further pressure to your stroke. Try playing familiar patterns but with dead strokes; this is a great way to vary a simple pattern. A dead stroke is notated by placing an "x" above the tab lines on the rhythmic notation.

▶ Palm Strokes

A variation of the dead stroke, drop a slightly cupped hand over the central note and allow it to rest on the surface, resulting in a punchy bass tone.

▶ Muted Tak

For added punctuation, try playing a tak while simultaneously muting the central note with a palm stroke using the opposite hand. This produces a sound similar to the tak, but with an added pop that creates a unique percussive texture.

▶ Note Muting

The natural long sustain time of a high-quality handpan allows freedom to experiment with muting notes. To do this, rest your hands back on a note or notes shortly after striking them. This can give an interesting character to a groove and can work particularly well in accompanimental roles.

▶ Note Waving

For a subtle wavering effect, wave a flattened hand perpendicular to the ground back and forth in the air above the ringing note. Doing this will deflect sound waves and modulate the note volume. Start slowly and increase speed. Emphasize this sound by waving closer to the instrument's surface. This technique is easiest on instruments with long sustain.

▶ Isolating Harmonics

The handpan is a unique percussion instrument in its ability to easily isolate tuned harmonic overtones. In any tonefield on a handpan, there are three distinct frequencies that sound when struck. By muting certain frequencies, the player can control which of these pitches we hear. As mentioned on page 7, each handpan note contains a fundamental pitch, an octave harmonic pitch, and a compound perfect fifth harmonic above that octave. To play an octave harmonic, you will isolate the octave by dampening the compound fifth harmonic and fundamental pitches. Place an index finger lightly on the ridge of the dimple along the axis of the compound fifth harmonic. Then, use your other hand to strike the note body near the edge and along the axis of the octave harmonic (Fig. 24). The octave harmonic should ring clearly because you have isolated it by muting the compound fifth harmonic and much of the fundamental frequency. If you hear nothing, you may be over-dampening. You may also need to adjust the placement of the dampening finger or your strike. Move in or out along the note body to find the "sweet spot" where the isolated harmonic is clearest. Sometimes the axes may not appear to be perfectly perpendicular. The sweet spot will be different on every note and on every handmade instrument. The steps above can be followed to isolate the compound fifth harmonic by switching the axes you dampen or strike. An octave harmonic played on a particular note is notated by the symbol "H8," while a compound fifth harmonic is notated by "H5."

Fig. 24: Isolating the octave harmonic by dampening the compound fifth harmonic

SEVEN-NOTE HANDPAN ETUDE NO. 2

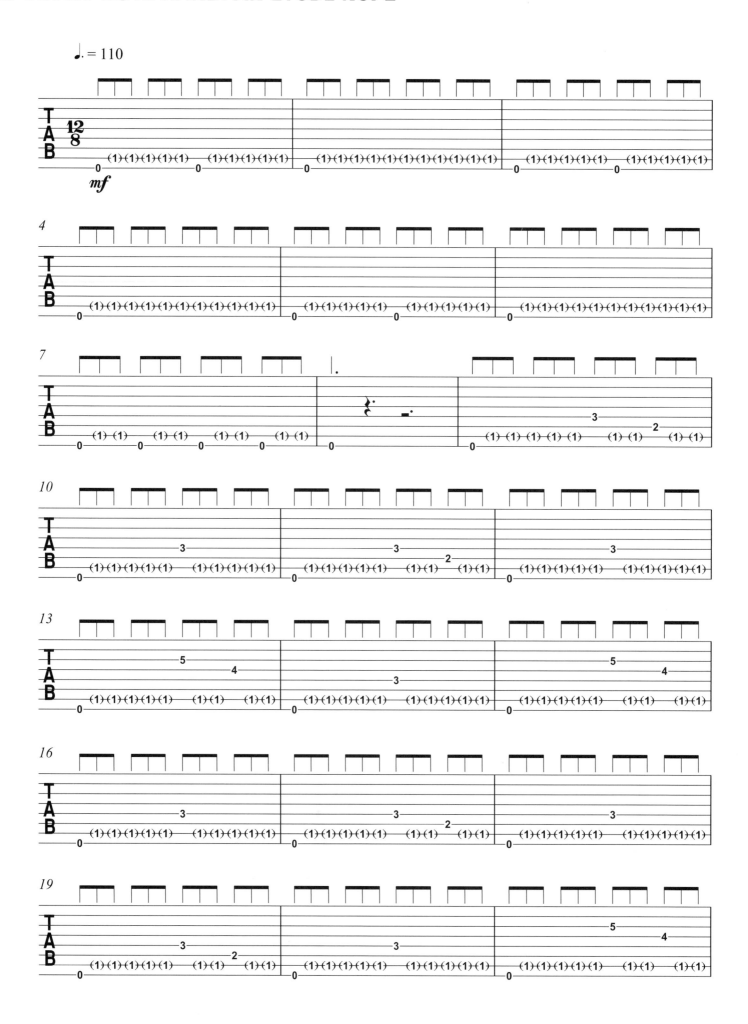

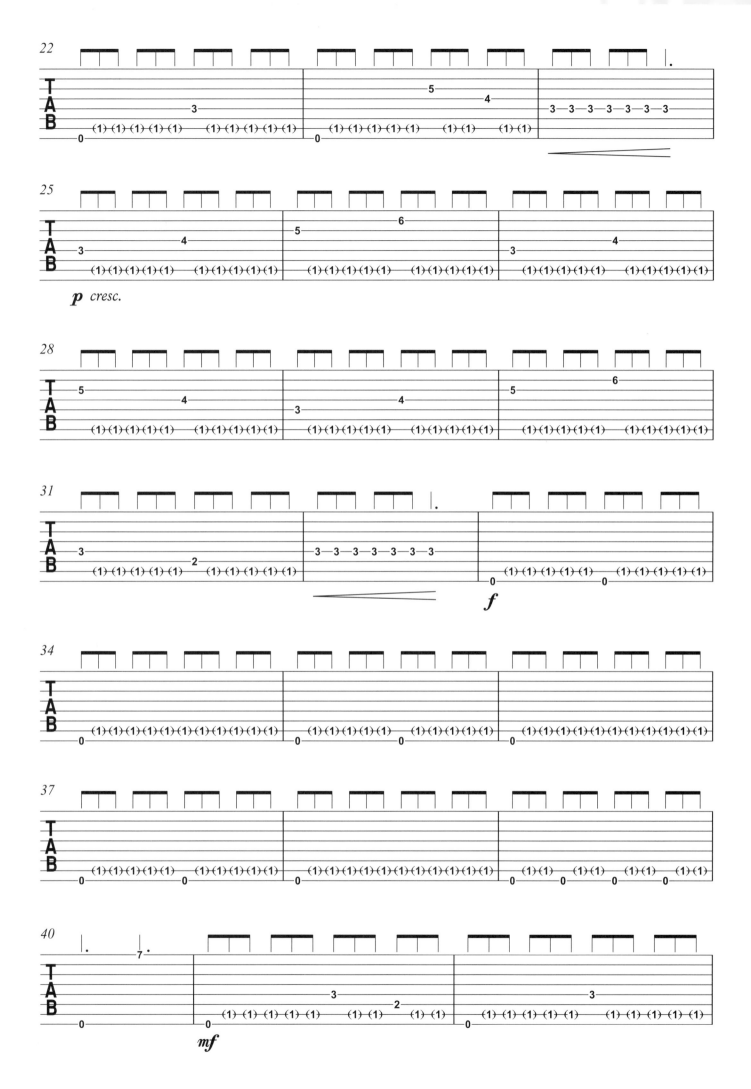

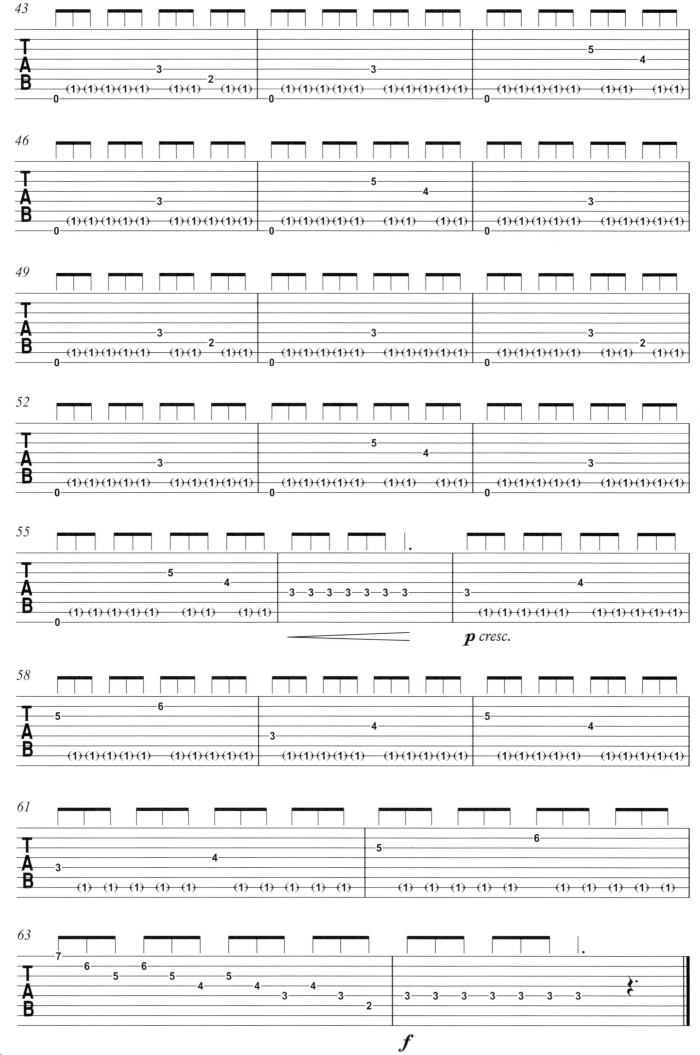

▶ EIGHT-NOTE HANDPAN ETUDE NO. 2

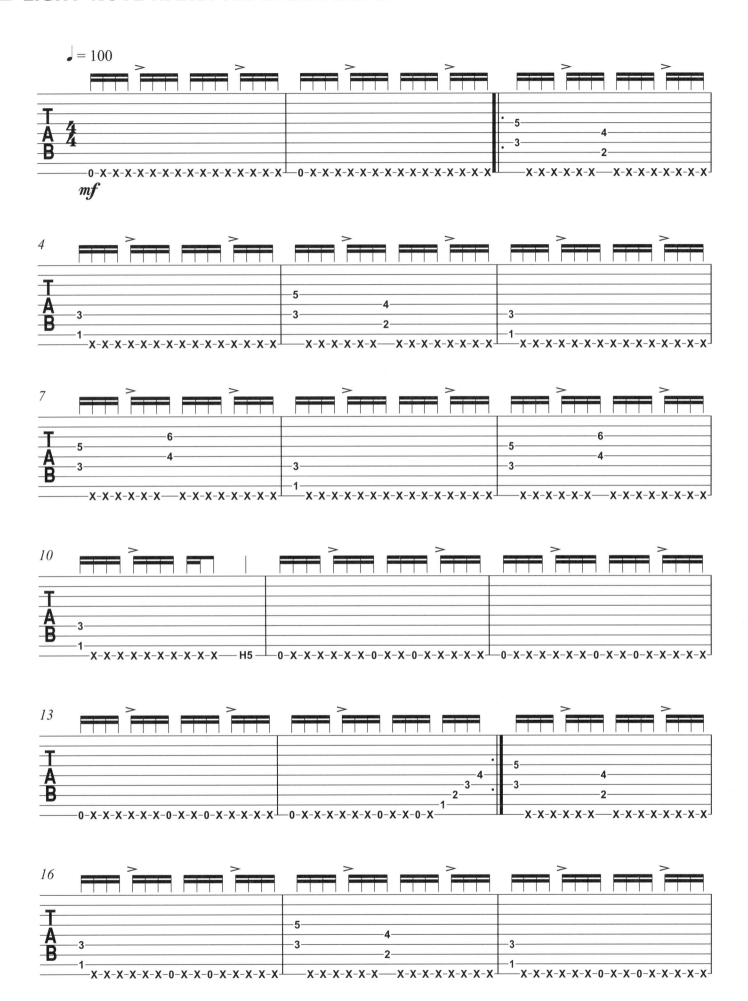

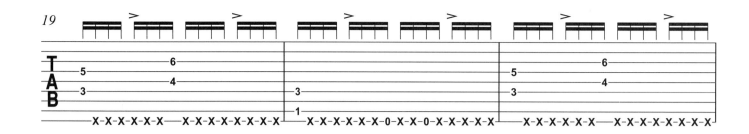

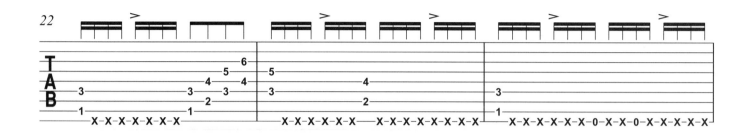

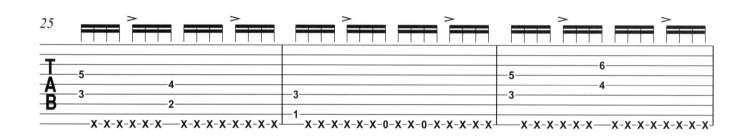

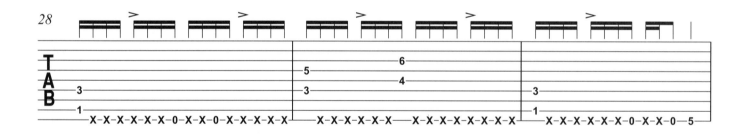

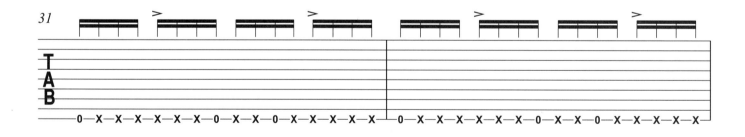

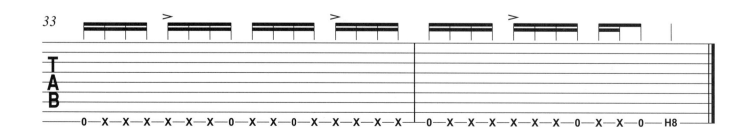

STAGE 3: COMPETENCY

- Master advanced playing techniques.

- Experiment with improvisation.

- Build structured songs.

- Develop your own voice and style.

ADVANCED PLAYING TECHNIQUES

The following are advanced playing techniques that come with some degree of risk to the instrument. Please proceed only when you know the limitations of your instrument.

▶ Isolating Harmonics with One Hand

Isolating harmonics with one hand requires you to dampen and strike as previously described, while using more than one finger on the same hand. Dampen one axis with the tip of your ring finger at the dimple edge while you strike the opposing axis with your index finger, aiming for the outer edge of the note body. To isolate the other harmonic, simply rotate your hand to mute and strike on the opposite axis. To achieve a clear harmonic sound, it is essential that your ring finger (muting finger) strikes the steel first; this should create a natural flam-type stroke. This technique will take some time and patience to learn.

▶ Pitch Bends

The handpan is capable of bending certain pitches, just like some stringed instruments. This is particularly useful on the central note. Start by isolating a chosen harmonic on the central note. As you strike, apply a small amount of pressure with the dampening finger; this will cause the pitch of the isolated harmonic to raise or lower. It is *essential* that you do not apply excessive pressure, as this may damage your instrument. This pressure should be gentle, light, and increased only after you execute a small bend, as you learn the limitations of your instrument. Experiment in finding the "sweet spot" where the harmonic resonates the fullest before you begin applying pressure. The sound of a properly placed pitch bend can add a unique and ear-catching color.

▶ Fist Strokes

For a bold, percussive sound, close your hand into a fist, with your thumb resting on top of your closed fingers facing upward. With a dead stroke, bring your fist down to connect the fleshy pinky side of the palm with a triangle of interstitial space between the central note and tonecircle on your instrument. It is essential that this stroke connects only with interstitial space, because a poorly placed strike could damage a tonefield. When executed properly, the result will be a deep thumping sound with a sharp attack.

▶ Activating the Helmholz

The handpan is a resonating chamber that can be activated by slightly changing the volume of the chamber and moving air out of the bottom port. To begin, lightly bend your hand upward at the wrist and use the soft area between your forearm and palm to carefully bump the dome of the central note. You should hear a low, rounded bass sound that comes from the port of your instrument. Alternately, you may group together a few fingers of the hand into a beak-like shape and tap the dome of the central note with the tips of your fingers. This sound can be particularly useful when playing vertically. You will notice that, as the size of the port changes, the Helmholtz pitch will raise or lower. You can experiment with this phenomenon by changing the diameter of the port with your hands or thighs.

HANDPAN MUSIC THEORY

The same concepts that apply to any other musical instrument apply to the handpan, though the handpan has a unique layout. This unusual design provides a new way of looking at chords, melodies, and other musical concepts.

Below is one of the most common handpan scales: a "Kurd" or "D natural minor" scale with eight notes (Fig. 25).

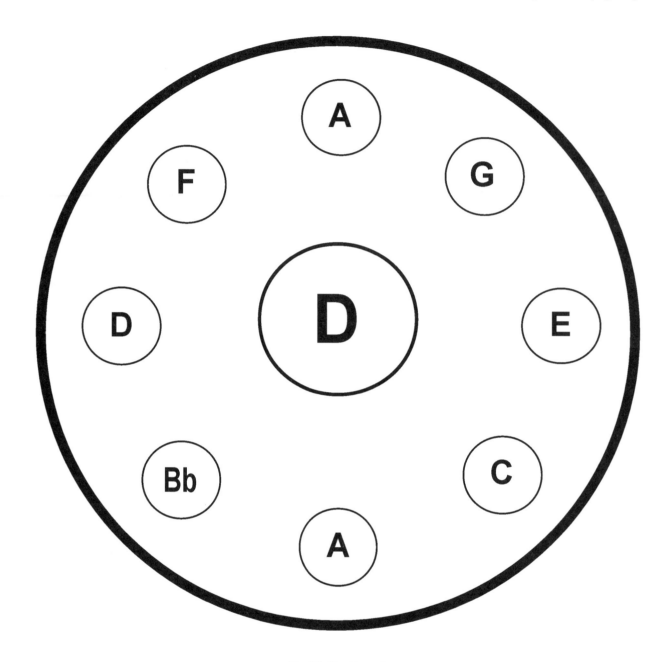

Fig. 25: Kurd layout

The Kurd scale is a particularly great example due to its diatonic layout. On most handpans, the central note is succeeded in pitch by the lowest note in the tonecircle, typically an interval of a third, fourth, or fifth. Subsequent notes then follow the scale pattern sequentially. Handpans with a complete scalar pattern illustrate one of the most unique concepts of the handpan, that of harmonic geometry. Following the standard zig-zag pattern, the movement is step-wise. However, when a player moves clockwise or counter-clockwise around the tonecircle, the intervals now occur in thirds. These neighboring thirds conveniently place chords in rows. On the Kurd scale, some of the primary chords alternate from the right side to the left side of the instrument. Starting at the bottom of the instrument, on the right side is the A minor chord (A-C-E), followed by the Bb major chord on the left (Bb-D-F). Then, a C major chord can be found on the right (C-E-G) followed by the D minor chord on the left (D-F-A). Adding a fourth note to each chord row creates seventh chords. Note the A minor seventh chord on the right (A-C-E-G), and the Bb major seventh chord on the left (Bb-D-F-A). Not all chords on the instrument will be found in rows like this. In particular, where scales omit pitches from the parent scale or have larger jumps between neighboring pitches, the chord geometry will change.

STRATEGIES FOR COMPOSITION

Harmonic Geometry

The harmonic geometry outlined on the previous page creates the opportunity for new approaches to writing music. Understanding and practicing the instrument's geometric patterns is one of the most helpful tools in writing music. If you find yourself repeating a pattern or chord progression and are looking to add variation, try playing the same grouping or pattern of notes after rotating the instrument to a new position in your lap. Treat the note facing the center of your body as your new note "one" (1). You are likely to discover a whole new world of harmonic and melodic possibilities. If you happen to have a second handpan in a different tuning, try adapting your favorite patterns and chord groupings that work well on one instrument to the other. The results might surprise you!

Sing!

Sing. It's one of the best ways to write enjoyable music on your handpan. Memorizing the pitches of your handpan will help you accomplish this. Use the following simple four-step exercise.

Step 1: Listening

Begin by slowly playing the notes of your instrument up and down the scale once, listening intently to the pitches.

Step 2: Singing

Ascend and descend the scale for a second time; however, this time sing or hum aloud the pitches of your handpan scale as you play them. (You may need to raise or lower pitches by an octave to fit your vocal range.)

Step 3: Internalizing

Play the up-and-down pattern of your scale for a third time, "singing" the pitches of your instrument internally, without making any vocal sound.

Step 4: Checking

Check to be sure you have memorized your scale pitches successfully. Before striking the central note to begin, hum or sing the pitch of the central note out loud. As you are still singing, play the central note to make sure the pitch you are singing is correct; adjust your singing pitch if necessary. Repeat this process for every note in the up-and-down pattern played previously.

A player who successfully follows the steps above will ultimately gain the skill to know what pitch a tonefield will produce, even before it is struck. When a player has achieved this, they are able to "sing" melodies internally (see Step 3) and their hands will know what tonefields to strike to produce these melodies… with no guessing.

PLAYING WITH OTHER MUSICIANS

The handpan's chromatic inability is one of its weaknesses. Since handpans are traditionally tuned to only one key, not every handpan will be able to be played tunefully with another, and other musicians can be limited in their harmonic material when playing with a handpan. However, the handpan is a versatile instrument and there are a number of strategies to employ when difficult harmonic situations arise.

1. Stick to the notes that work

It can be rare to find two handpans that are a perfect match. You can limit the notes played on each instrument to only those that are mutually harmonious. Using the Kurd (D natural minor) scale as an example, when paired with another handpan scale such as a D Dorian, you will notice there are many notes in common. To dodge a dissonant minor second, the Kurd player could avoid playing their Bb or the D Dorian player could sidestep their B♮. Those playing a Kurd scale with other musicians in the key of D major may want to steer clear of the dissonance produced by the F natural and C natural pitches of the Kurd scale. Omitting one of the dissonant notes is often the easiest way to improvise with another player. One need not understand music theory to make these choices. Experimentation can often tell you all you need to know. When playing with a partner, you can first determine and then avoid dissonant notes.

Kurd:	(D)	A	Bb	C	D	E	F	G	A
D Dorian:	(D)	A	B	C	D	E	F	G	A
D Major	D	E	F#	G	A	B	C#		

2. Play the port

If you find yourself in a situation where not a single note from your instrument will work harmonically, flip your instrument over to take a more percussive assignment in the music. You can model your role on that of a djembe, cajón, or another rhythm-based instrument player.

3. Get creative with additional sounds

In both of the previous strategies, you might find that your sound palette is becoming limited. Use this as an opportunity to explore some of the additional percussive sounds presented in Stage 2 and Stage 3 of this book. This can be a great way to add a splash of color to the music. You would be surprised at how many sounds you can create, even on one single note.

AFTERWORD

Congratulations! You have finished your introduction to the handpan. We hope the strategies provided in this book have given you a deeper understanding of, and stronger relationship with, your instrument. Finish off now with the following etudes.

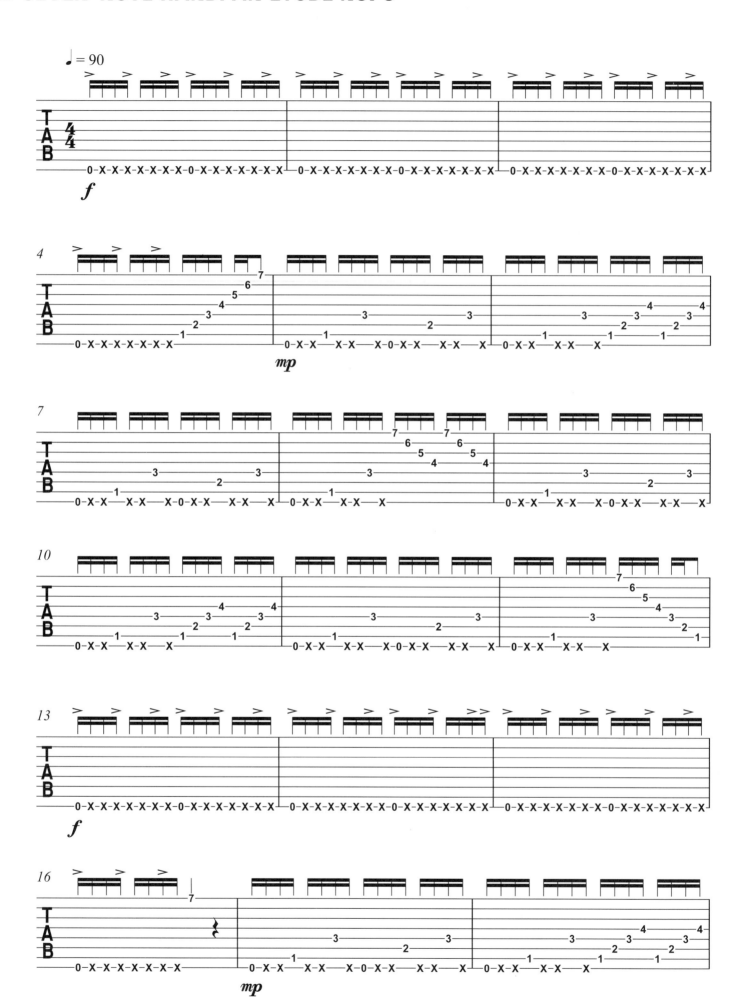

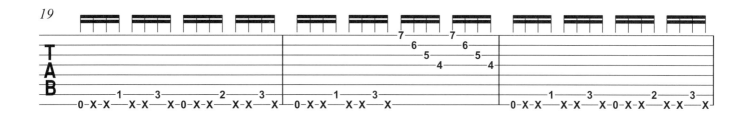

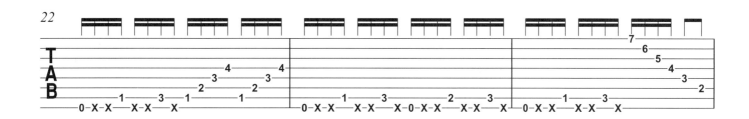

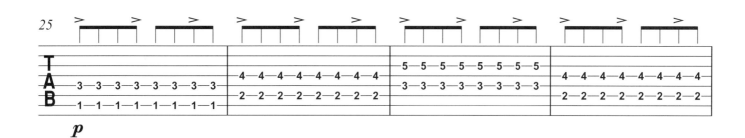

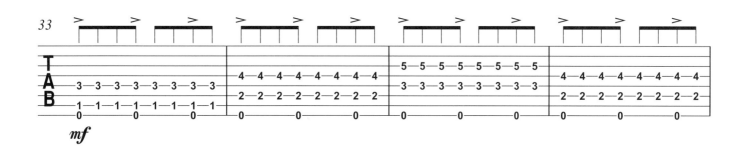

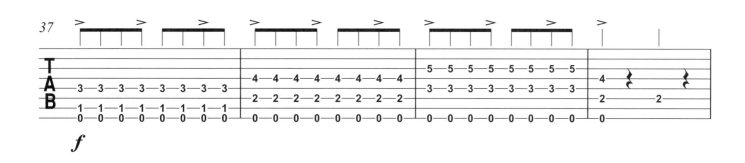

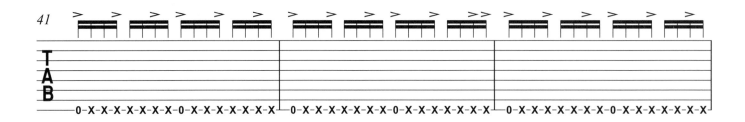

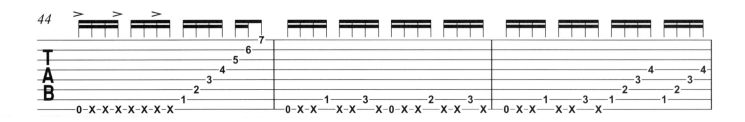

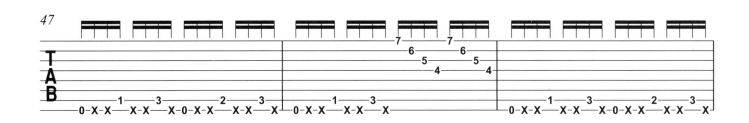

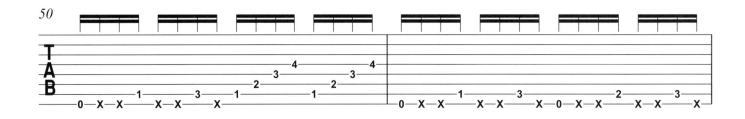

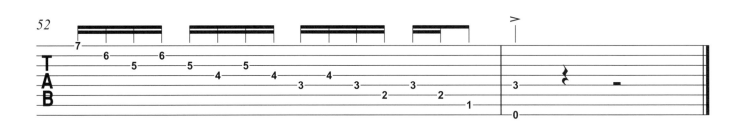

◉ EIGHT-NOTE HANDPAN ETUDE NO. 3

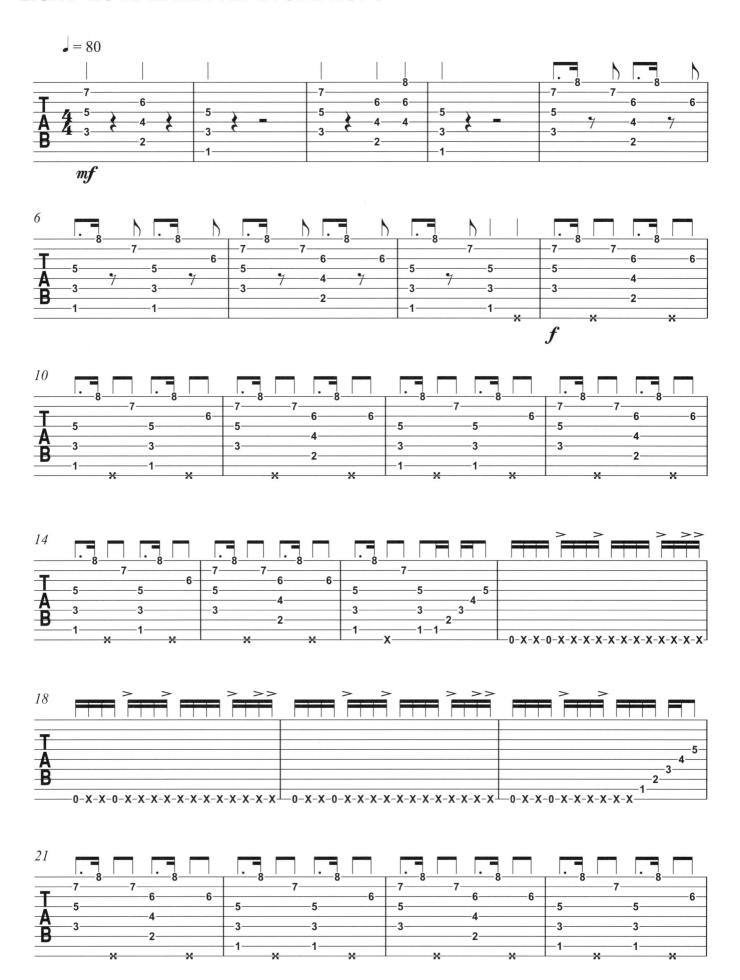

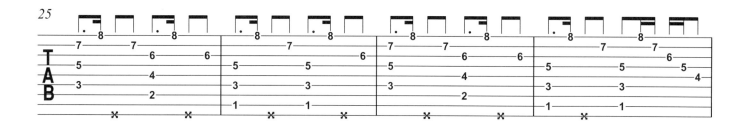

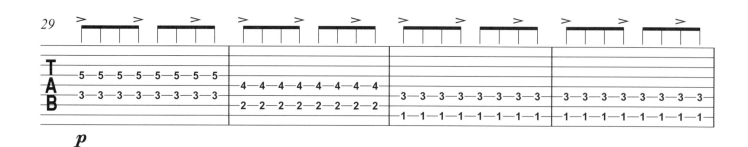

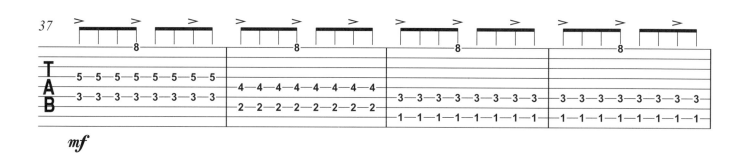

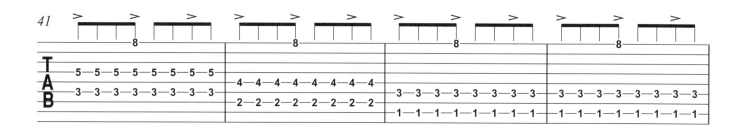

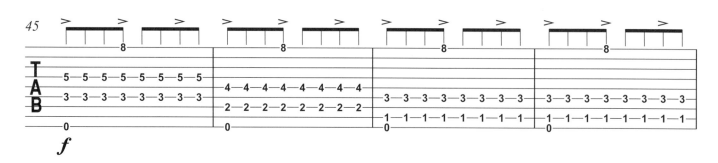

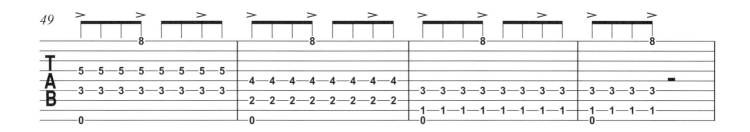

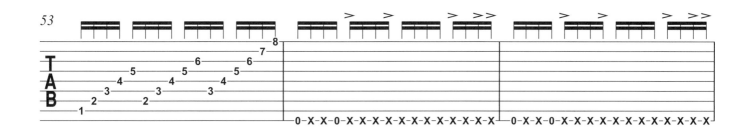

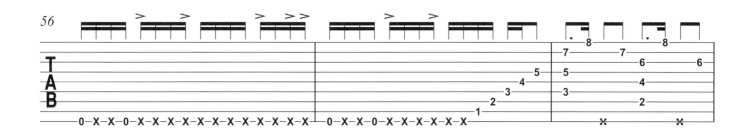

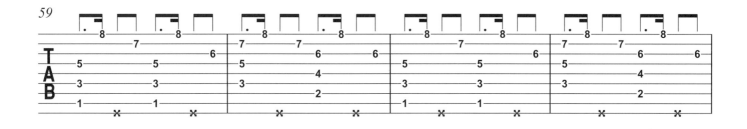

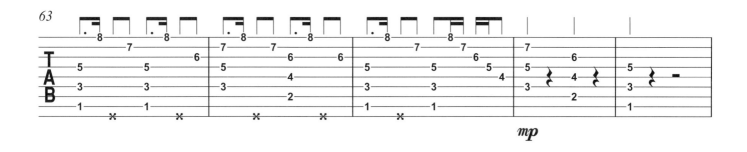

GLOSSARY

Activation: See sympathetic resonance.

Cavity resonance: The volumetric low bass-sounding frequency that becomes audible by forcing air through the chamber of the instrument. Also referred to as Helmholtz resonance.

Central note: The centrally located tonefield/note on the top of the instrument. It's most often the lowest note on the handpan and often the root note of the instrument scale. Colloquially known as the "ding."

Crosstalk: An adverse interaction of two or more pitches that causes resonation in a non-consonant way.

Dimple: The inward indentations in a tonefield.

Dome: The dimple of the central note. Domes can protrude inwardly or outwardly, can be circular or oval, and may have ridges.

Fill: A short melodic or rhythmic variation in a pattern.

Flam: A percussive **rudiment** of two strokes in which the first stroke is kept at a low volume and shortly precedes the second stroke.

Flange: See rim.

Ghost note: A stroke played at a very low volume used to fill out a groove and maintain a sense of rhythm among other notes.

Handpan scale: A series of notes, often with a unique name, that are partial expressions of a particular key, scale, or mode.

Harmonics: Overtones that accompany the fundamental pitch of a single note. Most handpan notes have a fundamental pitch, plus an octave harmonic and compound fifth harmonic.

Helmholtz resonance: See cavity resonance.

Impedance: A phenomenon occurring in handpans, due to the diameter or depth of an instrument, when certain pitches sound stifled or dissonant. This is caused by sound waves that do not properly align when reflecting through the shell. This can also be called phase shift, wave interference, or phase cancellation.

Interstitial: Empty untuned areas, found between the tonefields, ding, flange, and port.

Interstitial click: The percussive sound that comes from striking the interstitial space.

Nitriding/Nitrided: A heat treatment process that may create rust resistance, altered tone, and altered sustain. Not all handpans are nitrided.

Note body: The tone-producing region on the handpan that includes both the tonefield and dimple.

Port: The circular opening at the bottom of a handpan. Also known as the gu.

Rim: The flat metal that connects the top and bottom shells. Occasionally, the rim is covered with either a rubber or rope ring. Also known as the flange.

Rudiment: A combination of strokes that creates a larger pattern.

Shell: The concave metal semi-sphere that makes up a handpan. A handpan is comprised of two shells that are glued at the flange.

Shoulder: The area surrounding the ding where the interstitial and flat ding area meet.

Sustain: The length of time sound resonates.

Sympathetic resonance: The activation of one or more tonefields simultaneously on an instrument caused by the striking of a separate, complementary pitch. Also known as activation or bloom.

Tab: Abbreviation of tablature. Music notation system of lines and numbers, to communicate rhythm and note designations.

Tak: A high-pitched percussive sound played on the shoulder (outside edge) of the central note.

Tonecircle: The ring of tonefields that surrounds the central note of a handpan.

Tonefield: The elliptical flat areas found on the circumference of the handpan. These produce the notes of the scale when struck.

Tunings: See handpan scales.

ABOUT THE AUTHORS

Mark D'Ambrosio is a percussionist, composer, educator, and well-rounded musician from Colorado's Front Range. Mark specializes as a player of the handpan, a new and unique percussion instrument. He has performed as a soloist and taught throughout Colorado, the greater United States, Europe, and China. When not performing, Mark is an avid composer, arranger, and music producer; his music has received critical acclaim and has been featured in numerous creative projects. Mark's writings have been featured in such publications as the Percussive Arts Society's *Rhythm! Scene* magazine. Additionally, he serves as an educator for various area institutions in the Northern Colorado region and is a founder of the Steel Mountain Handpan Gathering, Colorado's largest handpan event. Mark holds a Bachelor of Arts degree in percussion from Colorado Mesa University.

Jenny Robinson is a handpan builder and tuner working in Madison, Wisconsin. She holds a Bachelor of Science degree from Northland College and a Machine Tooling Technics degree from Madison Area Technical College. In 2012, while working as a professional machinist, she developed a personal interest in the handpan instrument and began exploring the building and tuning process. In 2015, she started building full-time, merging her love of science, machining, and music in the founding of Isthmus Instruments, LLC, the first woman-run handpan company in the world. She is featured in several articles, including the article "Made by hand, played by hand" published in the *Wisconsin State Journal* (July 2016). She organizes the Midwest Handpan Gathering in Madison, WI to support the development of an interconnected community of handpan players. Her website: www.isthmusinstruments.com.